BEING ARAB

BEING ARAB

Samir Kassir

Translated by Will Hobson

with an Introduction by Robert Fisk

VERSO

London • New York

This book has been selected to receive financial assistance from English PEN's Writers in Translation programme, supported by Bloomberg. English PEN exists to promote literature and its understanding, uphold writers' freedoms around the world, campaign against the persecution and imprisonment of writers for stating their views, and promote the friendly co-operation of writers and free exchange of ideas.
www.englishpen.org

Liberté • Égalité • Fraternité
RÉPUBLIQUE FRANÇAISE

This book is supported by the French Ministry of Foreign Affairs as part of the Burgess programme run by the Cultural Department of the French Embassy in London. (www.frenchbooknews.com)

This paperback edition published by Verso 2013
First published by Verso 2006
© Verso 2006, 2013

First published as *Considérations sur le malheur arabe*
© Actes Sud Sindbad 2004
Translation © Will Hobson 2006
'Who Killed Samir Kassir?' © *Independent* 2005

1 3 5 7 9 10 8 6 4 2

Verso
UK: 6 Meard Street, London W1F 0EG
US: 20 Jay Street, Suite 1010, Brooklyn, NY 11201
www.versobooks.com

Verso is the imprint of New Left Books

ISBN-13: 978-1-84467-280-6

British Library Cataloguing in Publication Data
A catalogue record for this book is available from the British Library

Library of Congress Cataloging-in-Publication Data
A catalog record for this book is available from the Library of Congress

Typeset in Fournier by Hewer Text UK Ltd, Edinburgh
Printed in the US by Maple Vail

CONTENTS

Introduction

WHO KILLED SAMIR KASSIR?

ON JUNE 2 2005, the bloody hand has reached out to Lebanon once more, striking down one of its most prominent journalists and one of the most vociferous and bravest critics of the Syrian regime.

Samir Kassir was the best known columnist on the Lebanese daily newspaper *An Nahar*, a valued member of the opposition, newly married and - like so many of us in Beirut – living on the happy assumption that with Syria's troops and intelligence officers withdrawn from Lebanon, he had nothing to fear.

So who murdered Samir Kassir?

'He always left home at 10.30am and I saw him walking across the street,' a female neighbour told me on the day of Kassir's assassination. 'He always left home at the same time. He opened the door of his car, sat inside and started the engine. Then the car blew up.'

Close inspection of Mr Kassir's Alfa-Romeo, registration number 165670, showed clearly the blast came from beneath the driver's seat. It tore open the roof, blasted out the driver's door, smashed the steering column and hurled

Mr Kassir on to the passenger seat. The ignition apparently detonated the bomb.

It was a shock that no one in Beirut expected – except, of course, the assassins. In February 2005, Germany's top detective, Detlev Mehlis, had gone with his UN team to investigate the murder of the former prime minister Rafik Hariri. We all thought that Lebanon's assassins were in their rabbit holes, fearful of arrest.

But no, they are still on operational duty, still in killing mode. Nassib Lahoud, the opposition MP and friend of Kassir – he may be the next Lebanese president – was in tears when I spoke to him beside Mr Kassir's wrecked car. He talked about 'criminal hands', about the 'intelligence apparatus' who he blamed for the assassination. The only word he didn't use was 'Syria'.

So who murdered Samir Kassir?

Just before his resignation earlier in 2005, the pro-Syrian head of Lebanon's General Security Service, Jamil Sayed, hysterically offered to arrest himself if he was blamed for Hariri's murder. Mr Kassir had written a brutal article the next day, pointing out that it was good to see those who had threatened journalists and who had censored journalists now showing their own fear of justice. Rustum Ghazaleh, who was head of Syrian military intelligence in Lebanon, screamed abuse at the journalist.

So who murdered Samir Kassir?

In 2001, after a series of articles excoriating the Syrians and pro-Syrian Lebanese intelligence operatives, airport security confiscated his passport on his return from Am-man, claiming they wanted to 'verify the conditions upon which it was obtained'.

Mr Kassir was of Palestinian origin but had travelled on his legally issued Lebanese passport on fourteen recent occasions. In 2001, he complained he was under surveillance and his neighbours claimed they were interrogated by intelligence officers.

So who murdered Samir Kassir?

Nassib Lahoud had no doubts about the reasons for the murder. 'Criminal hands did not target Samir because he was a brilliant journalist,' he said. "They did not target Samir because he was a brilliant intellectual. They have targeted Samir for being one of the leaders of Lebanon's spring, because he was part and parcel of the opposition. So the battle with the intelligence apparatus is not over. This assassination is meant to tell us that Lebanon's march towards democracy should not be an easy ride.'

Mr Kassir, who had two children from a previous marriage, had only recently married Giselle Khoury, a journalist on the Arabiya satellite channel. 'Why don't they leave us alone now?' one of their young neighbours asked me. 'Why must they go on using this methodology of murder? We have to stop this. Are they trying to drive all the young people out of Lebanon?'

In the week before Kassir's murder, *An Nahar* had picked up a story that had been running in its rival paper, Mr Hariri's daily *Al-Mustaqbal*, and named three prominent Syrian intelligence officers who it claimed had - in defiance of UN Security Council resolution 1559 – returned to Lebanon to interfere in elections.

Identifying Syria's spooks is not a healthy thing to do. Their names were given as: Brigadier General Mohamed Khallouf – who was the senior Syrian intelligence officer in Beirut until last April - Nabil Hishmeh and Khalil Zogheib, who used to run Syria's secret services in Tripoli. Syria denied the men were here. Mr Kassir's last column – on the Friday before his death - was an attack on the Syrian Ba'ath party, headlined 'Mistake after mistake'.

So who murdered Samir Kassir?

Robert Fisk
3 June 2005

FOREWORD

IT'S NOT PLEASANT being Arab these days. Feelings of persecution for some, self-hatred for others; a deep disquiet pervades the Arab world. Even those groups that for a long time have considered themselves invulnerable, the Saudi ruling class and Kuwaiti rich, have ceased to be immune to the enveloping sense of malaise since a certain September 11.

The picture is bleak from any angle but even more so when compared with other parts of the world. Apart from Sub-Saharan Africa (the stage for an altogether different collision between potential and reality, expectation and achievement, anxiety and frustration, past and present), the Arab world is the region where men and, to an even greater extent, women have the least chance of thriving. 'Arab' itself is so impoverished a word that it's reduced in places to a mere ethnic label with overtones of censure, or, at best, a culture that denies everything modernity stands for.

Yet the Arab world hasn't always suffered such a 'malaise'. Apart from the supposed golden age of

Arab–Muslim civilization, there was a time not so very long ago when Arabs could look to the future with optimism. The cultural renaissance of the nineteenth century, the famous *nahda*, illuminated many Arab societies with modernity in a way that often went beyond the westernized, or westernizing, elites. In the twentieth century, one of these societies, Egypt, founded the world's third-oldest film industry, while from Cairo to Baghdad and from Beirut to Casablanca painters, poets, musicians, playwrights and novelists shaped a new, living Arab culture. These innovations were mirrored by undeniable changes in the social sphere, the most spectacular, revolutionary and now debated being women's decision to give up the veil. In politics likewise, the mobilization of societies enabled Arabs to play a prominent role in international affairs: Nasser's Egypt, for instance, one of the pillars of Afro-Asianism and the subsequent Non-Alignment movement;[1] independent Algeria, the driving force of the entire African continent; or the Palestinian resistance which was called on to further the cause of democratic rights without succumbing to the ideology of victimhood now so prevalent.

So what checked this momentum, which, even if it didn't achieve complete success, still heralded a better and seemingly attainable future? How did we become so stagnant? This state may be more intellectual and ideological than material but it still makes us believe that we have no future other than that proposed by a morbid fundamentalism. How has a living culture become discredited and its members united in a cult of misery and death? The following book aims to offer elements of a response to these questions and, by implication, to convey the possibility of finding a way out of the crisis.

This book makes no claim to be a political programme, nor for that matter the report of an expert witness. It is first and foremost the views of an Arab intellectual, such as could be put forward anywhere in the world: in Paris or Damascus, London or Beirut, Cairo or Casablanca, Algiers or – as has recently become the case – Baghdad. In saying this, however, I am not trying to hide behind a consensus of any sort. There is no consensus and every intellectual's own political identity informs his or her arguments. Before proceeding, therefore, I must first declare my identity.

The author of these reflections is an Arab from the Levant: secular, as will soon become apparent, acculturated, even westernized, but with no sense of himself as alienated from a foreign culture and no desire to eradicate those who think differently. He has no desire to try them in a foreign court either: this book has also been published in an Arab edition and, while this may not be a guarantee of universalism, at least it may be seen as demonstrating the possibility of conducting a debate that is both about Arabs and for Arabs.

Beirut–Paris, July 2004

I

THE ARABS ARE THE MOST WRETCHED PEOPLE IN THE WORLD TODAY, EVEN IF THEY DO NOT REALIZE IT

DO WE NEED to describe the Arab malaise? A few statistics should be enough to convey the seriousness of the impasse in which Arab societies find themselves: chronic rates of illiteracy, inordinate disparities between rich and poor, overpopulation of cities and desertification of land. You might say that this is the shared plight of a large proportion of what used to be called the Third World, and that, in any case, there's considerably greater poverty on the streets of Calcutta, for instance, or inequality in Rio de Janeiro. No doubt you would be right. Yet there's more to the Arab malaise than simply persistent underdevelopment, nor is it tied in with social class or even lack of education.

What's distinctive about the Arab malaise is that it afflicts people who one would imagine would be unaffected by such a crisis, and that it manifests itself more in perceptions and feelings than in statistics, starting with the very widespread and deeply seated feeling that Arabs have no future, no way of improving their condition. Faced with the protean and apparently incurable evil eating away at their world, the only remedy would be individual flight, if such a thing were possible. But the Arab malaise is also inextricably bound up with the gaze of the Western Other — a gaze that prevents everything, even escape. Suspicious and condescending by turns, the Other's gaze constantly confronts you with your apparently insurmountable condition. It ridicules your powerlessness, foredooms all your hopes, and stops you in your tracks time and again at one or other of the world's bordercrossings. You have to have been the bearer of a passport of a pariah state to know how categorical such a gaze can be. You have to have measured your anxieties against the Other's certainties — his or her certainties *about you* — to understand the paralysis it can inflict.

Still, you could conceivably overcome, or even simply ignore, the Western gaze. But how can you avoid returning it, and measuring yourself against its reflection? You don't have to go so far as to draw a comparison with a West that, while still the dominant global power, is based on a citizenship that is grounded in habeas corpus and human rights, and open enough to question and oppose periodic attempts by the state to control it. Nor need you despairingly contemplate that gulf between a civilization that constantly generates technological revolutions and your world, in which large numbers of people are still living in a preindustrial age, while the elite merely consume the innovations of other societies. More modest comparisons are astonishingly enough — with Asia, for instance, where economic growth has spawned a multitude of 'Tigers' and 'Dragons'. Or Latin America where democratic change appears to have acquired an unstoppable momentum. Or even Sub-Saharan Africa where, against all the odds, experiments in democracy coexist with traumatic civil wars. These regions, which until recently seemed to share with the Arab world a common fate of underdevelopment and authoritarian politics, are far from achieving parity with the industrial, democratic North, but they at least offer compensations which militate against despair. Some are making genuine steps towards democracy, others show economic growth or a degree of technological accomplishment that is the envy of Europe, others still are taking the initiative in international affairs — sometimes all of the above at once. By contrast, the Arab world suffers from a thoroughgoing lack of achievement in all these areas.

When you are thrown off course by the Other's gaze, or by the comparison of yourself to the Other, self-awareness is not a great help. The Arab sense of self has become so undermined that the slightest thing is enough to distort it. In some cases — and this is perhaps the Arab malaise's cruellest characteristic — one can feel innately deformed, without access or reference to anything outside onself. Admittedly, the deep sense of powerlessness at the malaise's core seems to be fuelled by unassuaged grief for past splendour. A historical paradigm appears to be invoked: Arabs' current impotence is all the more painful, the logic seems to be, because they have not always suffered from it; or, more precisely, the Arabs' malaise stems from their inability to regain the power and global status they once possessed. But unfortunately this doesn't accurately describe what Arabs feel anymore. Mourning past glories, which played such a part in modern nationalism and liberation movements, has ceased to be a spur to action. The Arab malaise has had such a debilitating effect that Arab history has been entirely hollowed out. What remains is a state of permanent powerlessness that renders any chance of a revival unthinkable.

The Arab people are haunted by a sense of powerlessness; permanently inflamed, it is the badge of their malaise. Powerlessness to be what you think you should be. Powerlessness to act to affirm your existence, even merely theoretically, in the face of the Other who denies your right to exist, despises you and has once again reasserted his domination over you. Powerlessness to suppress the feeling that you are no more than a lowly pawn on the global chessboard even as the game is being played in your backyard. This feeling, it has to be said, has been hard to dispel since the Iraq war, when Arab land once again came under foreign occupation and the era of independence was relegated to a parenthesis.

It's not important here whether you were for or against the war. For those who were against the American war on nationalist grounds – not to be confused with the millions of people who came out on the streets of Europe and America to publicly reject the United States' *diktat* – powerlessness is self-evident. It can be summed up in the simple, yet nonetheless bitter, acknowledgement that there was nothing they or anyone could do to prevent a foreign power – the greatest in human history though it may have been – deploying its troops thousands of miles from its borders to intervene as a policeman in your homeland, and in a matter of weeks put paid to a state that was much feared, at least by its own citizens and neighbours. Further proof of Arab impotence lies in the even more mortifying realization that if any opposition could have delayed the American occupation, it wouldn't have come from the 'Arab masses' but from the international civil society being put in place by the antiglobalization, or alterglobalization, movement, in which Arabs have only a very minor role. And even if the difficulties the American occupation is encountering have rekindled a certain nationalist fervour, those gratified by these developments know that they cannot count on any internal or regional assistance, only on their adversary's democratic capacity to affect policy. The nationalists therefore acknowledge that the occupation's outcome cannot ultimately depend on Arabs overcoming their own powerlessness.

As for those who were in favour of the war, powerlessness for them is a fundamental given. Whether complicit, opportunistic or a matter of their biding their time, their stance on American intervention arose from the conviction that the change Arab societies so badly need will not come from the people of the region: it can only be brought about with foreign assistance. But once provided, this assistance will not necessarily be empowering. Only those deluded enough to think that they are influencing events in their capacity as Eastern 'experts', or local informants, can fail to acknowledge that for better and for worse it is the victor, and the victor alone, who makes all the decisions. And in practice the successive haphazard decisions taken by America's imperial proconsul in Iraq can have only intensified Arab frustrations and aggravated their sense of impotence.

There's no doubt either that America's barely democratic actions have swelled the ranks of those who prefer the struggle against foreign domination to the fight for democracy, especially since the 'colonialist' critique of American domination in Iraq is underpinned by a general sense that the Americans were already working 'against us' anyway. We didn't have to subscribe to Islamist ideology to feel this: the United States' unwavering support of Israeli extremism was reason enough.

The American occupation of Iraq was by no means the first time Arabs have been beset by a feeling of impotence. Impotence has characterized the Palestine question at every turn, an impotence that has been all the more undermining because even the most knowledgeable of military experts cannot help setting it against the disproportion in size between the Israeli and Arab populations. There's no need to recite the commonplaces about the 1948 disaster, which was in fact far less unexpected than people make it out to have been. British general staff predicted it as early as 1946, because they knew, unlike the leaders of the semi-autonomous Arab states, that the Zionist Haganah outnumbered the entire Arab armed forces. One need not wax lyrical about Israel's exploits in 1956, which were only a qualified achievement that depended on the French air force and Nasser's shrewd decision to pull his army out of Sinai to defend Cairo, the real objective of the British, French and Israeli attack. Nor does 1967, which was an unqualified Israeli achievement, have to be a paradigm that damns Arab powerlessness as some sort of genetic or cultural flaw.

There was a strong vein of resistance and a determination to redress the situation during each of these episodes. The war of attrition waged by the Egyptian army after 1967 and subsequent crossing of the Suez Canal not only expunged any shame – to use a common register of Arab rhetoric – but also proved we Arabs could take our destiny into our own hands. Something we have never done since. After the half-victory – or half-defeat – of 1973, Israel has reigned supreme over the Middle East. Undeterred by Egypt since Sadat's peace, convinced of America's unfailing support, guaranteed moral impunity by Europe's bad conscience, and backed by a nuclear arsenal that was acquired with the help of Western powers and that keeps growing without exciting any comment from the international community, Israel can literally do

anything it wants, or is prompted to do by its leaders'
fantasies of domination.

The ultimate expression of the Israeli supremacy now
dictating Arabs' perception of the world and of their place
in it was the siege of Beirut in the summer of 1982. In their
first attack on an Arab capital, the Israeli air force put on a
special show. They carpet-bombed the city, hitting Beirut's synagogue, which was protected by Palestinian
fighters, throwing their planes through stunt routines
and even attempting to assassinate Yasser Arafat. On
one occasion they destroyed an entire apartment block in
a single strike with a vacuum bomb. In a tactic from
another age, the city was subjected to a total blockade and
deprived of food and water. Nobody in the world, neither
'Arab masses' nor oil diplomats, could stop this humiliation. When the city eventually gained some respite – of
the most basic sort; the water was switched back on – the
negotiating process by which it was secured was even
more indicative of Arab helplessness than the siege itself.
Petitioned by prominent Lebanese, the Saudi king had to
call the American president persistently before he could
get him to speak to the Israeli prime minister on their
behalf, which in turn more often than not came to
nothing.

These telephone calls are a good metaphor for the
effectiveness of Arab diplomacy in the Arab–Israeli conflict, at least in the aftermath of the 1973 war. Powerless to
change the status quo, the Arab leaders have gone to the
United States to ask it to moderate Israeli extremism, and

have met with practically no success, except in very circumscribed areas. Even on those rare occasions, America has conceded solely out of a desire to avoid aggravating what, from its point of view, was a critical international situation. This, needless to say, does not include the everyday realities of the Israeli occupation of Gaza and the West Bank, nor the constant colonization by Israeli settlements since 1967. As long as the status quo is unaffected, the United States isn't concerned that international law is permanently being flouted, as one can see from the number of draft resolutions it has vetoed on the UN Security Council. As for the resolutions that, when they have finally been watered down enough to get past Washington, quickly become meaningless documents — to say nothing of the countless futile resolutions of the United Nations General Assembly — these are even clearer proof of American indifference. Such diplomatic ineffectuality naturally intensifies Arab feelings of powerlessness. The more that's written taking Israeli policy to task or condemning it — the literature would run into volumes by now — the more starkly Arab helplessness is thrown into relief by the reality. The annexation of East Jerusalem, the constant chipping away at areas surrounding the city, and the settling of the West Bank and Gaza Strip: all have continued unabated since the signing of the Oslo Accord.

Faced with this degree of ineffectuality, neither the conviction that you are in the right and backed up by international law, nor the expressions of solidarity from all corners of the world, can compensate for the frustration you feel. The fact that you have all these advantages and yet cannot use them ends up transforming your feeling of impotence into some sort of destiny, as the business of the Israeli separation wall has once again shown.

Despite their apparent destinies, however, there are at least two peoples, the Palestinians and Lebanese, who have chosen to resist. The Lebanese can even pride themselves on achieving one of the rare Arab victories in the long history of the conflict. Achieved in two stages, their victory was all the more unexpected because theirs was one of the weakest countries in the Arab world and at its lowest ebb. Initially a broad front, in which the left played the most active and effective part, the resistance quickly forced Israel to give up Beirut – the birthplace of opposition at the start of the occupation – and then, after three years' constant fighting, to evacuate the main towns in the south of the country. Once Israel had abandoned its plans to make Lebanon a satellite state, the occupation began to take its toll. With the revival of the resistance at the end of the 1980s this became too heavy to bear, although it took Hezbollah, who had the monopoly on resistance from then on, over a dozen years to liberate the country. But it also took its toll on the Lebanese – having been in control of their resistance to the Israeli occupation, they allowed themselves to become subservient to Syria's tactical manoeuvrings – and on the Arabs as a whole. From then on resistance was an Arab totem, conceived of and advocated as an end in itself, distinct from politics.

Resistance became a model to be exported regardless of circumstances, with Palestine its first destination, although the balance of power there was quite different and the occupier far more prepared to make sacrifices to maintain the status quo.

The Palestinians' predicament is therefore far greater than that faced by the Lebanese and yet nothing seems able to reduce them to despair. Their capacity to endure hardship and always bounce back could be an example to all Arabs. But the Arab ideology of resistance can't envisage everyday heroism of this sort. Despite a political elite that has become very skilful in balancing international affairs with the regional status quo, the perception of Palestine – by the Arabs more than by the Palestinians – remains unaltered. The Palestinian movements may have been responsible for the call to 'total guerrilla war' at the end of the 1960s. However, it is the opinion-makers of the other Arab countries who have imposed 'total intifada' on the Palestinians since the great uprising of 1987–89, so that they end up being treated as a people of professional revolutionaries whose courage consoles and cathartically appeases the consciences of those who watch from afar, applauding in front of their TV sets.

But whether Lebanese or Palestinian, resistance serves only to highlight overall Arab powerlessness. The second intifada, which started in September 2000, bears this out day after day. The hold of the concept of 'total intifada' is such that any analysis lays one open to accusations of treason. The idealization of resistance per se, based on a misunderstanding of the situation in Lebanon, prohibits any debate on the means that should be employed and so gives precedence to the most spectacular. Even if, like the suicide attacks, they are the most counter-productive. The Islamization of the Palestinian struggle, despite yielding sporadic gains that flatter the Arab public's wounded pride, hardly arrests feelings of Arab powerlessness or counters the overall impression of general malaise. It has had quite the opposite effect in fact: the blurring of Palestine and Iraq has been of no help to either, and merely swamped the self-image of the Arabs of the Middle East – and the image the world has of them – in a tide of blood.

It has to be said that this powerlessness is not a cause of despair for all Arabs. There is an active, and apparently growing, faction that regards it as a secret cause for exultation, and as legitimizing acts of apocalyptic or at best Samsonian violence. The adherents of radical Islam are not really worried at all, in fact. Even the denunciation of the Western 'crusade' has for them the merit of confirming the superiority of the victims; all the latter then have to do is claim their victimhood and thus ascend to paradise.

This religious reflex is itself a sign of the Arab malaise. Of course, considering political Islam as one factor of the Arab impasse may be seen as fanatically secularist. If they have changed, there's no need to insist on judging the Islamists by their past conduct, and by the fact that they played the Americans' game, and in Palestine the Israelis', for far too long. Everyone is entitled to change and one should no doubt concede the possibility that the Islamists' transformation is permanent and their stand against foreign domination sincere. But this is still not enough to make one accept Islamism as the only possible way. For whether if is or is no longer a foreign agent, Islamism still reinforces the Other. In justifying, or enacting, the clash of civilizations, it gives supporters of the crusade their rationale and enables the West to use all the means afforded it by its technological capabilities to maintain its supremacy over the Arabs, and thereby to perpetuate Arab powerlessness.

II

A DEEP SENSE OF MALAISE
PERMEATES EVERY CORNER
OF THE ARAB WORLD

SOME PEOPLE IN Europe, and even in the Arab world, might consider the picture I have painted of the Arab malaise as itself a sign of the crisis, in so far as its presupposition of a global Arab entity smacks of pan-Arabism. One school of thought, inspired by American neoconservatives, maintains that the persistence of Arabism is one of the causes of the Arab world's backwardness. This is most improbable. The picture would be no more cheering if one were to consider each Arab country separately. Admittedly, a tracking shot of this atypical continent would reveal some contented Arabs, and others who are aspiring to be so, but it would also show at every turn societies in crisis and deadlocked states, all ill-equipped to take their futures into their own hands.

Painful though it may be, it is worth conducting such a review of the Arab world, and Egypt, which has long played a pivotal role in it, is an obvious starting point. In the overpopulated Nile valley, with its vast economic disparities, the Egyptian state displays a chronic inability to manage its country's human resources, let alone play a role beyond its borders. A hypertrophied bureaucracy blocks the workings of an economy that combines the worst of both worlds: the disadvantages of state capitalism, once rashly called socialism, with the failings of ultra-free-market economics. Emblematic of this sclerosis is the highest office of state, which has been held by the same man for twenty-three years, a record of longevity unsurpassed since Muhammad Ali in the nineteenth century.[2] At least he initiated the country's modernization and set in train decisive reforms, the effects of which were felt for over a century. His successor shows no such ambition, nor, oddly enough, does he even portray himself as a hero, unlike his predecessors – perhaps because he knows that the real power lies with the military, from which he came, which is itself another sign of the impasse. Such 'modesty', however, hasn't prevented either the personalization of the regime or the extensive practice of nepotism: accusations of wheeling and dealing have been levelled at the president's elder son for years, while certain political and economic circles openly lobby for his younger son to inherit office. But Egypt's impasse is not merely a matter of governance. The whole society, including the elite, seems so in thrall to an ideology of stagnation that the few voices of protest are easily co-opted by the regime to become stooges of a pseudo-democracy. Meanwhile Islamism looms large: fuelled by a popular religious revival and indulged by the government, it has been spreading for years, veiling women and closing minds in ever increasing numbers.

To the south of Egypt, the Sudan, having barely emerged from a twenty-year civil war, now threatens to descend into a new one. Scene of an extraordinary squandering of natural riches, this colossus of the African continent and the Arab world is one of the least advanced countries on the planet. This in itself should sum up the stasis in which it is mired. Despite the end of the civil war, its integrity as a state remains in jeopardy, since the agreement that concluded hostilities explicitly allows for the possibility of the animist, Christian-dominated South breaking away after a transitional phase. Not to mention the immeasurable damage it has done to Arabs' reputation in black Africa. Not content with having oppressed the South, the Arabized, Muslim North now gives allegedly out-of-control militias carte blanche to persecute the people of Darfur.

To the west of Egypt, Libya has been frozen in Gadaffism for thirty-five years. The global populism of the 'guide of the revolution' has alienated it from the international community and caused it to fall out with most of the Arab states. Oscillating between the Levant, the Maghreb and Africa, Gaddafi's Libya has ended up abdicating any claims to be a regional power in return for a certificate of good behaviour dramatically conferred on it by a West at war. Its isolation is far from over, however, since the *soi-disant* 'regime of the masses' has produced a political vacuum in a closed society under constant police surveillance.

Further west, each of the three principal countries of
the Maghreb after their own fashion offers equally dis-
piriting images of the Arab impasse. Morocco has embarked on its democratic transition too late and only to a
limited extent. Reined in by the palace, the multiparty
system hasn't even been able to reduce the hoarding of
wealth that is embodied by the Makhzen system,[3] which
has meant the party of government, the former opposition, losing its credibility. After a brief improvement in
the press, freedom of information has once again got short
shrift. Unalleviated by political progress, problems of
underdevelopment fuse with the rhetoric of militant Islam
to produce networks of jihadists, which then spread to
other countries. In Tunisia, Islamism is kept in check for
the moment by the police, who use their power to take the
entire society prisoner and silence any democratic expression or criticism of the mafia-type corruption that is
feeding on the country's economic growth. This authoritarianism has in turn fostered a culture of tacit dissent
among the working class – and elsewhere – that distorts
the genuine social achievements of Bourguibism.[4] But
Algeria is undoubtedly the most dramatic embodiment of
the Arab predicament, and perhaps the most resonant,
more so even than Egypt, because it was once such a
symbol of promise.

Having been one of the pillars of the Arab world,
Africa and the Non-Alignment movement for two decades, Algeria, although its leader still symbolizes that
dynamic period, has seen its political role shrink drama-

tically at both a regional and a global level, while suffering catastrophic internal upheaval. Like Morocco, the 'socialist' excesses of Boumédianism[5] served as a pretext for the class in power to enrich themselves, while after a misguided change of course the economy proved itself ever more incapable of sustaining an expanding democracy, despite considerable oil revenues. The ensuing loss of faith in the political process soon allowed a revival of militant Islam, to which the ruling military found no answer other than repression, which in turn led to civil war. Fortunately Algeria has emerged from this, and reclaimed freedom of speech in the process, but it is still dependent on a regime that only has a civilian façade and, crucially, lacks any real prospects, something for which all the president's media and diplomatic experience is far from compensating.

Looking east of Egypt, to the Levant, the picture becomes even bleaker. The havoc radiating out from the Iraqi inferno alone should convey the extent of the impasse the Arab world has reached. Iraq unites the three ills obstructing the future: dictatorship – and what a dictatorship, still traumatic even after its fall – foreign occupation and, thanks to the occupation's blunders, a wave of blind violence that justifies itself in the name of religious messianism. Instead of Iraq growing into the Arab Prussia it showed signs of becoming in the 1930s, the extraordinary squandering of its riches threatens to turn it into a second Somalia. Arabism has degenerated from a source of optimism to a stain on Arab identity, which it will take a long time to remove.

A stain that Syria, its neighbour and Baathist twin, continues to compound. Suffocated for forty years under a dictatorship that, although less bloodthirsty than Iraq's, has still brutally run it into the ground, systematically bled dry by powerful mafias, and weakened by a culture of fear, Syria is now in a position almost without equivalent in the Arab world – apart perhaps from Libya, although it doesn't have Libya's oil – in that it combines the corruption of the former Soviet republics with a Chinese-style closed police state. Bordering Syria to the west and still in its shadow, thanks to its intelligence services, Lebanon has embarked on a unique regression. Having barely emerged from a war that tore its society apart and deprived the Arab world of one of its laboratories of modernity, Lebanon has in the fifteen intervening years forfeited most of the advantages that had long set it apart, starting with an open, resourceful media. Certainly it can pride itself on having liberated its territory from Israeli occupation through the resistance of its people – or part of its people – but now even that achievement has been appropriated by Syrian obstructiveness and Islamist activism. Not to speak of the republican tradition that had managed to survive the war, however grievously wounded.

Paradoxically, of all the Arab countries of the Near East, it is Jordan, without any natural resources or democratic tradition, that seems to be doing best. But a perennial obsession with security hampers its halting transition to democracy, and the influence of parliamentarism has so far been confined to providing a platform for the most sterile populism, thereby reinforcing conservatives' and tribal groups' opposition to any improvement in women's rights. At the same time Jordan's geopolitical position, next to the two centres of instability, Iraq and Palestine, raises the question of its durability as a state, especially since Palestine feels like a permanently open wound every day to its population, over half of whom are Palestinian refugees.

The picture might appear superficially more attractive if one turns to the Arabian peninsula. I do not of course mean the Yemen, which carries no echo of any *Arabia Felix*, real or fictional, of old. One of the least advanced countries in the world, its unification – between the tribal, militarized North and the Marxist, ex-colonial South – has resulted in women's rights, one of the few achievements of socialism, being challenged and produced a regime that controls and manipulates a nominally pluralist system, while compromising with lawless regions run by breakaway tribes and groups of jihadists.

I am thinking, rather, of those countries on the other side of the peninsula where societies previously untouched by developments of any kind in the Arab world have been utterly transformed by the black gold in the space of two generations. So much so that some people have started to think that the Arab world's future, particularly when globalization is increasingly geared around the Pacific, may lie in the luxury emirates of Qatar, Dubai, Abu Dhabi and, to a lesser extent, Bahrain.

It's impossible not to be impressed by the metamorphosis these countries have undergone. In Dubai, where skyscrapers proliferate in a cityscape worthy of Chicago, the titanic programme of development and modernization has even managed to impact favourably on the climate – irrigation and green spaces have caused a drop of two degrees in average summer temperatures. But beneath these obvious, showy successes lie elements of a grave instability. The structure of the populations and the restrictions imposed on citizenship, for a start: most people living in the emirates are foreigners, Arabs and otherwise, who have no political rights nor any prospect of ever acquiring them through naturalization. At least half of the nationals live in conditions of scandalous inequality by virtue of the circumscribed status of women, still generally covered from head to toe – except when they go to Beirut on holiday. In the case of Bahrain, there is also the religious issue, in which the Shia are relegated to the status of second-class citizens.

A still greater threat facing this string of rich emirates is the fact that modernization remains merely window dressing. The dominance of tradition, symbolized by the fetishization of national dress – and the obligatory veil – stifles social change. The same people who swear allegiance to the global economy are often responsible for financing that other global enterprise, jihadism. Qatar is an obvious case in point: despite the American military presence there, the Islamist faction in the ruling family is so strong that it could engineer a Muslim Brotherhood takeover of Al-Jazeera. Kuwait is an even more striking example: the country owes its survival entirely to America's protection but, like Jordan, its revived parliamentarianism only intensifies opposition to the modernizing legal change the Americans supposedly want.

Of all the threats to the principalities of the Persian Gulf, however, the most dangerous is the instability of their vast neighbour, Saudi Arabia. Along with Egypt, Algeria and Iraq, the Saudi kingdom has the potential to be one of the centres of the Arab world. While lacking the other countries' cultural depth or a political tradition in which to articulate a leadership role, the immense wealth it has accrued from oil has allowed it to exercise a real influence over the entire Arab world since the 1970s. It is now a giant in crisis. Oil revenue allowed the kingdom to acquire a modern infrastructure in record time, but now it is no longer enough to satisfy the growing needs of an increasingly complex state, the ever more sumptuous lifestyle of the House of Saud's seven thousand-odd princes and a population whose poverty is no longer out of sight.

Before September 11, Saudi Arabia appeared to be confronted by an urgent need for reform, on the one hand, and on the other the impossibility of implementing any reforms without upsetting the delicate balance between the Sauds and the religious establishment. Quarrels between the matrilineal sub-clans of the ruling family and the advanced age of the most influential princes pointed to a succession crisis which it was hard to see being resolved without a coup, possibly with foreign backing. September 11 has added an unprecedented sense of persecution to this mix, as the Saudi elites have watched the West, led by the United States, close its doors to them. Since then Saudi Arabia has found itself caught between the necessity of reform, now an urgent demand of America, and the mounting confidence of the jihadis, who are indulged and protected by the religious establishment, from which the government refuses to dissociate itself. The escalation of terrorism, which has only been belatedly countered by the government and enjoys considerable support among the population and the state apparatus, now threatens a scenario like Algeria, although with more chaotic consequences, given the fact that Qur'anic literalism is the ideology of everyday life.

This is undoubtedly an incomplete picture, but it nonetheless allows us to pinpoint the other major failing of the Arab world besides its impotence in international affairs – its democratic deficit. Lack of democracy may not be a specifically Arab problem, but the Arab world is still the only region where virtually every country suffers in this regard. Actual dictatorship may be confined to just two countries, Syria and Libya (Iraq's being of recent memory), but it casts its shadow over them all and, by setting the context for pseudo-democracies such as Jordan, restricts genuine political participation. Nor has citizenship gained enough authority in any Arab country to drive democratic change. But it would be a mistake to impute the crisis of citizenship to any cultural predisposition. The real crisis in the Arab world is the crisis of the state.

The state is experiencing a crisis of one form or another in almost every single Arab country. The first, and perhaps most serious, symptom of this upheaval is the recurrent phenomenon of states' internal unity being challenged. Lebanon has been spared this, but it is looming in Sudan, and now a country like Iraq, which has long been considered durable, is threatened. On a smaller scale, other countries have suffered violent expressions of internal groupings, either along the lines of religion, *asabiyya*, such as in Bahrain, the east of Saudi Arabia, Syria and even Egypt, or distinctive ethno-cultural identities such as in Algeria.

An equally alarming, although less obvious, symptom of the crisis is institutions' general lack of popular credibility. There is good reason for this: none of these states has shown any continuity in institutional matters. On the contrary, if there has been a marked tendency since independence, it has been that of institutions progressively losing substance.

In countries which at one stage or another have followed a 'socialist' path, the struggle for national liberation has perversely tended to remove all trace of the legally constituted state from the governing elites' thinking, even though some of the foundations of such a state date back to the last decades of the Ottoman era.

Economic liberalism has not made much difference; if anything, it has made things worse, as one can see from the erosion of the independence of Egypt's judiciary, which was comparatively protected under Nasser. In other countries, monarchies that have demanded direct loyalty to the king haven't even needed a concept of citizenship until recently. The best an Arab opposition can therefore hope for is a more restrictive version of the Mexican model of democracy – that is to say, a regime that permits a certain degree of freedom of expression while offering no real possibility of a change of government. This is demonstrably the case in Egypt, Jordan, Lebanon and Morocco. But these half measures are inadequate to produce a genuine political process, as Algeria has shown. It took this route between 1988 and 1992 before the experiment had to be stopped because it was out of control. The deadlock the Egyptian regime seems to be in today is another example. It goes without saying, of course, that a modicum of free speech is a long way short of a legally constituted state. Any factions that are considered a real threat to the regime in power tend to be denied it anyway. One cannot therefore speak of 'citizens' in countries where the ruling powers, republicans though they may be, see only subjects.

Another symptom of the crisis of the state, which probably has the most potential significance for the Arab world, is the tendency of governments, voluntarily or otherwise, to relinquish sovereignty in economic and financial matters. The question of sovereignty, apparently so significant when it comes to explaining the futility of plans for Arab integration, goes out of the window when the world order is involved, or when integration involves non-Arab countries, as in the talk of 'complementarity' and 'normalization' which was a feature of Arab–Israeli negotiations in the 1990s.

In this sense, the political dysfunction in all the Arab states, whatever their regimes, plays a part in perpetuating foreign hegemony, in the same or almost identical way as the manipulation of debt and control of economies paved the way for the West's political and military hegemony in the nineteenth century. This tendency, discernible before September 11, has been thrown into fresh relief by the 'War on Terror' and to an even greater extent by the Iraq war. In many respects it represents a return to classic colonial domination, not just in Iraq itself, but also in the Gulf states where the American bases, unlike in Turkey, enjoy extraterritorial status, and elsewhere. Many national police forces – even that of the easily offended Syria – now receive training from the FBI.

The only 'continent' where all its members suffer from the democratic deficit, the Arab world is thus also the only one where the lack of democracy is allied to a foreign hegemony, generally indirect and purely economic, but in the most extreme cases – Palestine and now Iraq – resembling a new colonialism. Consequently the feeling of impotence fuelled by this domination is coupled with a civic powerlessness, which is all the more overwhelming because the Arab unconscious filters it through nostalgia for a forgotten but still fantasized-about glory. Not only can the current regimes not give, or restore to, their states the ability to take the initiative in international affairs; they also forbid their citizens any licence – if not to change these regimes, then at least to breathe new life into them through popular participation, or at the very least create a popular solidarity that could defuse any external threat as it arose. Instead, whether it's called Israel or the United States, this threat is used as a pretext for a permanent state of emergency that moves, with complete disregard for the law, to neutralize politics and ban all its regulatory mechanisms, starting with parties and associations. The crisis of faith in the political process then runs its course, until there is nothing left but religion to channel people's frustrations and express their demands for change.

Although today militant Islam appears primarily to target the West, it was initially a product of the impasse in Arab states. Saudi Arabia is an exception, since its political and religious establishments have been blurred since the kingdom's founding. But everywhere else the rise of political Islam took the form of a reislamization of society in response to what were considered to be inefficient, iniquitous, or impious, governments, rather than a reaction to the culture of modernism. Obviously the Iranian revolution played a role, giving the religious revival an anti-Western cast and then passing this on to Arab Islam through the Shia in occupied Lebanon. But the Sunni version of political Islam didn't adopt this anti-Western

stance for a long time, at least r
Afghan jihad left the former muja
free to choose a new enemy. 1
meanwhile, reislamization concentr
nal politics.

As a product of the democratic de
rise could only be a response to the cr
and the deadlock of Arab societies. A   ...sistance to
oppression, it also arose from the failures of the modern
state and the broken egalitarian promises of progressive
ideologies; in this sense, it resembles the rise of fascism in
Europe. Indeed, once the religious veil is removed the
societal attitudes of the Islamist movements reveal many
similarities with fascist dictatorships. If one is to admit
political Islam's claim to be a force for change therefore,
one must accept that the democratic deficit is permanent
and that the Arab world will never make its appointment
with modernity.

As a constituent element of the Arab malaise, the
illusion that political Islam could offer a way out of
the crisis is striking. Generally speaking, we shouldn't
forget either that the focus of religious thought, even
before bin Ladenist jihadism, is a regression in the literal
sense of the word — that is, in terms of Arab history.
Contemporary Islamism in fact wants to do away with all
Arab history, recent and classical alike, in order to recover
the forty or so years of 'pure Islam'. But it's only when we
can recover this history in its entirety, that we will be able
to envisage an end to the Arab malaise.

III

THE ARAB MALAISE IS A PERIOD OF HISTORY AND IT IS NOW MORE ACUTE THAN IT WAS BEFORE

THERE IS GENERAL, unhesitating agreement on classical Islam. Apart from a few racists clutching their half-understood copies of Voltaire, one no longer finds any reasonably cultivated person who would dispute that Islam in its first flourishing between the 7th and 11th centuries CE was, to quote Maurice Lombard, one of the most fertile chapters in the history of civilization. Bernard Lewis, the most authoritative – although by no means the least perverse – critic of contemporary Arabness, takes this as his starting point to ask what went wrong.

These past glories, however, particularly when harked back to in a way that begs the question of Arab history in general – or amounts to special pleading – can shine so brightly that they obscure everything since. After its 'golden age', Arab history is viewed as no more than a string of failures, a single continuum of misfortune. No mention of the fact that later periods had their share of achievements and success, both political and military as

well as cultural. Strangest of all, no word of a recent past
that seemed to be overflowing with promise. Even forty
years ago, any survey of the Arab world would have been
largely optimistic; the Arabs seemed as if they were on the
move, an integral and at times leading part of the Third
World revolution.

It must be said that this neglect is encouraged by Arab
perceptions of their own history. Leaving aside the
Islamist factions (the only golden age they allow is the
forty or so years under the Prophet and his first four
successors, the rightly guided caliphs, after which there is
nothing for them but regression towards a state of
ignorance), the main school of Arab historiography,
established by the original twentieth-century Arabist,
Syrianist and Lebanist nationalists, divides Arab history
into three periods. Arab historiography owes a general
debt to European models, whose direct influence is
particularly clear in this case. Just as in European thought
the splendour of Antiquity gives way to the night of the
Middle Ages, so the Arab golden age yields to a long age
of decadence (*asr al-Inhitat*) before the renaissance (*nahda*) arrives. Debatable in itself, this tripartite structure is
also dated, in so far as the *nahda* is now considered to be
over. Worse still, due to the endemic lack of historical
memory that is the curse of contemporary Arab culture,
people are forgetting that this failed renaissance had even
taken place. All that's left of Arab history is decadence
without end and a golden age that can never be recovered.
Whereas in the recent past, when the renaissance still

seemed within reach, the prominence of this glorious past set up a tension that was predominantly creative, it has today become crushingly oppressive since the alleged failure of the Arab renaissance.

Perhaps the first thing we should do, therefore, is to free ourselves of this millstone – not by denying the glories of Arab civilization under the Umayyad and first Abbasid dynasties[6] (and their continuation in Andalusia) but by situating them in a history stripped of religious predestination, on the one hand, and nationalist teleology, on the other.

Religious predestination clearly shapes the canonical version, which holds that the history of the Arabs starts with the revelation of the Qur'an, and skirts over everything before as a time of chaos, or *jahiliyya*, the Age of Ignorance. Poetic narratives and tribal myths are the only record one finds in post-Hegirian Arab history of the century or so of the *jahiliyya* leading up to the Prophet. Yet this image of anomie does not tally with recent Roman and Hellenistic historical scholarship. The latest findings in archaeology, epigraphy and numismatics show, among other things, that the Arab cities north of Hijaz[8] were not only completely Roman, but the birthplace of several Roman emperors. This dents the romantic image of purely nomadic, warrior ancestors that has fired the post-Hegirian Arab imagination – we can only imagine the Copernican revolution that would be brought about by the discovery of a golden age before the Golden Age.

Freeing Arab history from the grip of religious predestination, therefore, entails deislamisizing its beginnings; refuting nationalist teleology, on the other hand,
involves recognizing how much more important Islam
was than ethnicity as a unifying bond in its subsequent
phases. Within three decades of being galvanized by
Islam, Arab history has merged with the history of the
other peoples incorporated into the Muslim state – and
subsequent Muslim states – to form a culture in which
religion is but one among many shared values. With this
in mind, it is much harder to assert the idea of this
culture's decadence without at the same time denying the
reality of its golden age and all that period's imaginative
worlds.

The golden age would itself gain from being reap-
praised from this perspective. Any comprehensive assess-
ment of these five centuries would require volumes; but
for present purposes, two fundamental aspects of the
period that need to be emphasized are the international
presence Arabs enjoyed and the gift for synthesis they
displayed. Politically, this meant world-power status and,
at the same time, regimes flexible enough to accommodate
ethnic and religious diversity at every level, and to do so
on a scale comparable only to the Roman Empire.
Culturally, it meant universality and plurality. Arab
society was able to absorb the cultures of the Islamized
peoples and not negate them in the process. Whereas the
hitherto dominant Byzantine civilization had remained
isolated from its Hellenistic roots in general, and from

Ancient Greek science and philosophy in particular, the new Islamic culture brought about a revival of classical thought, initiated by the Hellenized elite of Syria and then taken up by Islamic thinkers, who went on brilliantly to develop its concepts and disciplines themselves. This has too often been seen as purely conservative, as marking time until the cultural baton could be handed on to Renaissance Europe – a view that belittles not only the entire intellectual history of the Christian Middle Ages, which was steeped in Arab thought, but also the demonstration of universalism hereby provided by Islam. Like the Church Fathers before them, although in an entirely different way, the Arab philosophers did not just appropriate classical philosophy, but also set out the universality of reason. Those who claim that Arab democracy is a theoretical impossibility would do well to consider this precedent.

Universality, mark you, not uniformity. The cultural community – the Arab *universitas*, as it were – revolved around a host of urban centres of cultural production, and drew on a web of diverse 'sub-regions', each with its own anthropological sensibility, or specialization. This geography by no means always matched that of the numerous mini-states that flourished and gave way to one another during the second Abbasid age.

Then, after the Abbasids' power was weakened still further, came the notorious 'decadence'. Accelerated by the invasions of the new barbarians, the Crusaders and the Mongols, the advent of the Arab Middle Ages is traditionally symbolized by the Mamluks, those praetorian slaves who had held the reins of power since the tenth century but only assumed it openly at the end of the thirteenth century.[9] People tend to forget that the armies of Islam ended up repulsing both the Crusaders *and* the Mongols and that the Mamluks played an even more decisive role in these victories than Saladin. The Mamluk era was without doubt a period of religious intolerance – principally directed at Shiism – and its image will always remain blighted by the repressive abuses committed by the army rabble and the ceaseless round of palace revolutions, particularly under the Burjits, the Circassian Mamluks. Nevertheless one cannot ignore the undeniable achievement of its Baroque architecture, which is the antithesis of the very idea of decadence, or the fact that it saw the rise of Arab encyclopaedism and the birth, at the hands of the great Ibn Khaldun, of the discipline that was yet to be called political sociology.[10]

Next came the Ottoman era, which marked the real restoration of Muslim power after the hiatus of the Crusades.[11] Turkish culture now took precedence; Arab culture was subordinate – equal, in many cases, with its Greco-Byzantine counterpart. If it would be stretching a point to speak of the Mamluks in terms of decadence, it is simply untenable to do so of the Ottoman state, which crowned the long Muslim quest for Constantinople with glory and supplanted the Byzantine Empire. This is no less true of its culture, as one can see from the marvels of Ottoman architecture, not just in Istanbul but also in many Arab cities, and from the current re-evaluation of its formalist poetry. From now on, Arab culture shone through individual works, but particularly as part of a larger imperial culture. The Empire's ethnic diversity produced an intermixing of populations which is still evident in families' lineages, even if it is sometimes masked by a rather bizarre genealogical purism, as well as exchanges of ideas and traditions that revealed themselves in the technology of work and the culture of daily life.

In its imperial phase, Arab history reads like an accumulation of cultural experiments or, more precisely, as an accumulation of cultural diversity. This is hardly surprising, given that its legacy is still the basic point of reference – and legitimization – for the most divergent systems of thought. Primacy of the profane over the sacred for some, of the sacred over the profane for others, philosophical rationalism, theocratic authoritarianism, dissenting mysticism, even utopianism – nothing human is alien to the Ottoman Empire's cultural universe. Rebels and men of power, philosophers and Sufis, preachers of every stamp, from the most visionary to the most conservative – all casts of mind coexist and succeed one another over its long history. Jostling and interweaving, it embraced schools of thought as diverse, and at times as antagonistic, as the Aristotelian rationalism of Averroes, on the one hand, and the theology of Ghazali on the other; or again, the prototypical sociology of Ibn Khaldun and the Qur'anic literalism of Ibn Taymiyya.[12] Whether these were Ancients modern before their time, or Moderns still attached to the past, the fact is that their ideas have largely retained their authority at the start of a new millennium.

Putting the notion of decadence into context does not mean closing one's eyes to what may appear to be a grave deficiency of Arab culture at this point (but only if one compares it exclusively with the globally dominant culture of the last two centuries). This shortcoming, shared by Ancient Greek and Hindu civilizations, is of course technological. But here too we need to put things into perspective, and recognize the undeniable technological advances Arab society made in a number of domains, such as medicine, optics, and navigation systems. Furthermore this technological deficit was only later of consequence: during the Renaissance, the Muslim world more than held its own against Europe. The Ottoman Empire, which dominated its Muslim and Christian rivals by its command of artillery, remained a superpower of the old world for two centuries. Lepanto may have been a victory for the Venetians and the Spanish, but the euphoria with which it was greeted clearly shows which way the balance of power tilted at the start of the battle.[13] And despite its outcome, to which European historiography gives undue importance, the warring fleets in the Mediterranean remained equally matched for a long time.

A technological gap did not begin to open up until the second half of the eighteenth century. The decline of the

Ottoman Empire coincided with the Great Transformation, the collection of changes that paved the way for the Industrial Revolution, the modern market economy and the modern nation-state in Western Europe. Coincided is the word, since there was absolutely no causal relation between the two phenomena – not at that period, at any rate. The Russian Empire that began to push back the Ottomans wasn't caught up in the capitalist ferment; in many respects, it was significantly less modern than the Ottoman state; and while the decline of the Ottoman army was palpable against the Russians, Al-Jazzar was still able to turn back Bonaparte at the gates of Acre.[14] The economic aspects of the Great Transformation were far more devastating; combined with Russian expansionism, they created the 'Eastern Question' – but not before the end of the eighteenth century. The beginnings of the unequal exchange across the Mediterranean and, after the Napoleonic Wars, the expansion of European trade then caused the Muslim world to fall behind at an exponential rate. Meanwhile, the chain reaction of the French Revolution ended up exposing the Empire to the centrifugal forces of nationalism.

But even in the face of the irresistible rise of the industrial, colonial West, the Muslim East was not slow to respond, albeit in imitation. In Egypt Muhammad Ali, nominally the Ottoman governor but in practice an autonomous head of state, set about modernizing the administration, for the purposes of which he sent scholars to be educated in France, rationalizing agriculture and instigating a preliminary phase of industrialization. This spirit of change then spread to Istanbul, where the Ottoman elite in turn embarked on a great project of legal and administrative modernization. Thanks to the programme of reform known as the *tanẓimat*, the reorganization, the old Empire changed totally in three decades – dress included – so much so that it became (even if just for two years) a constitutional state. All the advantages of technological civilization – railway, telegraph, electrification, steam navigation – were adopted east of the Mediterranean pretty much at the same time as they were in the north. Daily life was transformed in Istanbul and the large urban centres of the Arab provinces alike, and a parallel cultural revolution put the Ottoman elites in sync with Europe. This is the revolution Arabs have called the *nahda*, although they have tried to isolate its meaning and the change it represented from a nationalist and then explicitly anti-Turkish viewpoint.

It is uncanny how this relatively recent era plays less of a part than other more distant periods, either in the way the Arabs are perceived or in the way they represent their own history. Muhammad Ali's modernization is forgotten; the work of the *tanẓimat* is forgotten – or else only seen as part of Turkish history; above all, the *nahda* is forgotten, except perhaps by an elite that is still attached to the spirit of the Enlightenment. Yet it would be impossible to exaggerate the benefits of restoring this era to its proper place in Arab history. It may perhaps not reveal tailor-made formulas for putting an end to the malaise, but at least it would allow one to reinterpret this malaise as a moment in history. If Arabs don't reclaim this history, their relationship with modernity in the twenty-first century will remained warped by misunderstanding.

IV

MODERNITY WAS NOT THE
CAUSE OF THE ARAB MALAISE

NOWADAYS, IT IS verging on intellectual blasphemy to talk of 'Arab modernity'. But the fact remains that denying the success of this experiment, even if we must consider it now predominantly to be over, implies a contempt for Arab cultural and real – that's to say lived – history. Of course we need to agree on a definition of such a quintessentially volatile word. In the West, postmodernism invites us to look at modernity as dated and hence to define it as a historical phenomenon. If one tries to define it anywhere else, though, one cannot avoid the debate on the relationship between modernization and Westernization – a less obvious debate than may at first seem the case. One school of contemporary Middle Eastern studies, for instance, regards Islamism as an attempt to appropriate modernity. But for the moment let's accept the narrowest definition, whereby modernity is understood solely in terms of the Western model, following the bourgeois revolution. If one can show that the Arab world adapted to this model, that Arab modernity was an historical and lived reality, then there cannot be an intrinsic difference between Arab and Western cultures. A culturalism of difference could only be an excuse for present failings. The obvious place to begin testing this thesis is the Arab nineteenth century. If we do not simply gloss over it – as Bernard Lewis does, for instance – a very interesting equivalence between modernization and Westernization soon becomes apparent in the Arab world.

As aspects of Arab modernity, I have already mentioned the programme of political reform initiated by Muhammad Ali and taken up and developed by the Ottoman rulers, as well as by Khayreddin in Tunisia,[15] and the gradual but nonetheless swift adoption of the advances of technological civilization. To these we should add patriotism in Rousseau's sense of the word, the French Revolutionary ideal that gave rise to Greek and Serb, then Turkish, Armenian and Arab nationalism, the second wave being fuelled by the apparent success of the first as well as by the debates over Italian unity.

Without it being developed to this degree, we can see the patriotic ideal in embryonic form at the time of Muhammad Ali, when it was espoused if not by him then at least by his son Ibrahim Pasha. Ibrahim, who conquered Syria with the help of the famous Suleyman Pasha, veteran of the Grande Armée, and administered it for a decade, explicitly placed himself 'under the sun of Arabness', despite being of Albanian extraction.[16] This was also the time Rifaa al-Tahtawi gave the word *watan* (homeland) the modern meaning he discovered in Europe.[17] Accompanying the first scholarship boys sent to Paris by Muhammad Ali, Tahtawi returned with the *nahda*'s founding work in his bags, the *Gold of Paris*, which is not simply a far more truthful *Lettres Persanes* but also an unambiguously modernist profession of faith by a reformer from a religious background. Unlike his present-day successors, Tahtawi saw no incompatibility between modernity and the tradition from which he came. Three decades later, Butrus al-Bustani, the other great pioneer of the *nahda* – it had reached Beirut in the meantime – adopted Tahtawi's ideas to formulate an Arabic-Syrian patriotisms that stopped short, however, of rejecting Ottoman citizenship.[18] Along with Bustani, other notable figures of the *nahda*, including the cosmopolitan and unclassifiable Ahmad Faris al-Shidyaq, explained their work as lexicographers in patriotic terms, by their love of their language, as if anticipating the linguistic nationalism that was still to come.

All of this shows that the *nahda* had an intrinsic nationalist dimension. This became more explicit in the poetry of Ibrahim al-Yazigi before emerging fully formed in the founding works of political Arabism. The *nahda* was thus both an Arab cultural renaissance and the first stirring of Arab nationalism, similar to the crystallization of Italian patriotism. It was, as it were, a combination of the European Renaissance of the fourteenth and fifteenth centuries and the Risorgimento, but without an armed uprising or a Kingdom of Piedmont to articulate it. Egypt, which could have played this role, was penned within its borders by the vicissitudes of the Eastern Question and the Great Game once Ibrahim Pasha's adventure in Syria had been brought to an end.

It is a short step from the nationalist aspect of the *nahda* to an Arab nationalist reading of the history of Islam, according to which the three periods – Golden Age, Decadence and Renaissance – refer only to the Arab peoples. But such a reading profoundly obscures the diversity of this cultural revolution, the range of modernity it introduced. Patriotism and nationalism, totally new ideas in the Arab world at the time, certainly show that the main Arab centres were part of a universe of political modernity from the nineteenth century onwards – but there was far more to the modernity of the *nahda* than that.

The first way nationalism distorts the history of Islam is, as I have said, to force it into a straitjacket of three periods. Apart from making no sense in terms of literature, the 'decadence' overlaps at least in part with the golden age of the Ottoman Empire, which despite an irresistible decline could still command the allegiance of the majority of the Arabs at the start of the First World War. Even more importantly, the European historiographical model misrepresents the *nahda*'s historical and cultural inspiration. Rather than the European Renaissance, the *nahda* modelled itself on the Great Transformation of the eighteenth century. Both in its content and in its modes of expression, the *nahda* was the child of progress and the Enlightenment. It laid claim to the entire legacy of the French Revolution, which was infinitely more wide-ranging than simple patriotism. So one can see how nationalism, by distorting the *nahda*'s intent, managed to marginalize the values of universality, liberty and the inviolability of human rights advocated by many Arab authors, and to discard every aspect of the Great Nation posited by French revolutionary thinkers except the concept of nationalism. Similarly it reduced the concept of liberty to that of national liberty, without regard for individual liberty, even though individuation gathered momentum in the Arab world in the nineteenth century much as it did in the West, chiefly as a result of the revolution in transport and the urban explosion.

A second distorting effect of nationalism is that it erects territorial barriers around the *nahda*, reducing it to a purely Arab phenomenon. The extraordinary effervescence of ideas that characterized the renaissance would have been unthinkable without the dynamism shown by all the ethnic groups of the Ottoman Empire, starting with the Turks themselves. In fact, the thirst for enlightenment was nowhere expressed more vigorously and effectively than in Istanbul, where it culminated in real reforms that not only modernized the administration and legislative corpus but also represented the first steps towards establishing a legally constituted state and constitutional practice. Once again the distortion is retrospective. At the time, the spirit of reform and the transformation of the

Empire's legal structures swept up the social elite in every Arab city of the Empire. Furthermore, despite the constitution's thirty-year suspension under Abdul Hamid,[19] the *nahda*'s legalist conception of the strong state, supported by the image the Europeans projected of their systems, seems to have had enough impact for all the Arab states formed after the dismantling of the Empire to acquire constitutional and parliamentary structures based on the nineteenth-century model of formal democracy. And yet no one remembers this whole sweep of history. Even more destructively, democracy is now said to be incompatible with the Arab psyche or tradition because its first incarnation failed.

The final distortion that comes from this type of ideological reading is a tendency to link the outcome of the *nahda* to that of nationalism. The *nahda* is thus thought to have failed because the 'awakening' of the Arab nation did not play out. Worse still, because it did not lead anywhere politically, it is considered not even worth remembering; and everything it explored – progress, the individual, how to modernize Islam – should be discarded with it.

Nationalist teleology does have its limits, however. Despite the deadlock paralysing Arab modernity, the word *nahdawi*, man of the renaissance, still has favourable connotations, rather like humanist in Europe, as does *tanweeri*, man of the enlightenment. In other words, the *nahda* remains an attitude, like the European Renaissance (a good comparison, for once) and the Enlightenment, which was its true inspiration. This should in itself be an incentive to re-evaluate the *nahda* in terms of what it actually was, rather than what it should have been.

With the *nahda*, Arab culture reconstructed itself on the basis of the discovery of the Other, the European Other. It wasn't always easy. The exchange remained one way, and took place in the shadow of the confrontation between East and West – hence the considerable frustrations that have charged contemporary Arab history with tension and steeped it in an irreducible anxiety. Yet it was also through this confrontation that the principles of Arab modernity were formed.

Far more than Japan, where modernization concentrated on reproducing the technological, military and financial mechanics of the West's supremacy, the Arab world, nowadays described as inherently closed, embraced all the intellectual debates that came from Europe. It wasn't slow to do so either: less than a half century separated the appearance of the first feminist theories in Europe and Bustani and al-Shidyaq's appeals for the advancement of women (the latter also calling for women's right to pleasure in a way that was revolutionary even in the context of nineteenth-century European thought). After socialism's emergence as a political force in Europe, the same al-Shidyaq wasted no time in inventing a neologism, *ishtirakiyah*, to translate it. When Darwin died, it took only two months before two young Beirut intellectuals risked inciting an evolutionist war –

which incidentally only brought them into conflict with
the American pastors at their university and the French
Jesuits in charge of the rival establishment.

The transformation was phenomenal. Arab culture,
with the Ottoman Arabs to the fore, threw itself into a
prodigious programme of adaptation, translation – in a
word, modernization. The rule was passed over everything, including religion. Today's Arabic still bears the
traces of this transformation in its numerous simplifica-
tions, neologisms and 'barbarisms', which are predominantly French.

Refashioned by a host of nineteenth-century lexicographers, translators and polymaths, contemporary Arabic
reflects the integration of the Other in obvious ways, such
as its technical neologisms, and much subtler ones, such as
its semiotics. Astonishingly, one of the modernizing
influences on the sacred language of the Qur'an was
the Bible's translation into Arabic. Naturally the Christian
missions – Protestant and Catholic – financed this project.
There were three rival versions, and it was local Chris-
tians, including once again the formidable Bustani and al-
Shidyaq, who did the bulk of the work, but nevertheless a
Muslim religious dignitary was involved in one version.
The contribution of a Muslim scholar of the stature of
Sheikh Youssef al-Assiir to this Christian undertaking is
undeniably one of the most powerful and moving signs of
the humanism of the *nahda*.

Arabic also sought out the new by incorporating
literary genres from outside the Arab tradition. Both

through translation and original work, Arab prose ex-
perimented with theatre, autobiography and in particular
the novel. But it wasn't just writers and translators. What
turned this historical phenomenon into a cultural revolution was the accompanying transformation in society.
Accelerated by greater educational opportunities – not
just missionary schools but also those run by the Ottoman
public authorities and local private schemes – a new
socialization was encouraged by a range of associations
and the emergence of a highly diversified press. Before
universities, scholarly societies were the forum for in-
novative thinking and the latest intellectual developments. They conducted the most extensive and varied
debates: on scientific discoveries, the virtues of commerce,
the struggle against superstition, women's education,
historical analysis, rationalism – everything that seemed
liable to stimulate society and help it make up for lost
time. Most of the newspapers shared this aim, loudly
proclaiming their allegiance to progress while helping to
disseminate the neologisms and simplified form of the new
Arab prose.

This colossal metamorphosis met, as we have said, with
reservations. But it would be a mistake to infer from them
a fundamental opposition between modernization and
Islam. In Beirut, the Muslim association of the *maqassed*
began its charitable and educational mission by opening
two schools for girls, while many Muslim notables did not
hesitate to send their children to missionary schools. The
great Muslim reformers are the best indication of how

unfounded such an opposition is. While preaching Islamic
resistance to the West in Arab circles in Egypt, and then
Paris, the Persian Jamal al-Din al-Afghani was a confirmed rationalist.[20] His disciple Muhammad Abduh, who
was to become the Mufti of Egypt, subsequently applied
this rationalism in writings that were Islam's key modernizing texts – a genuine *aggiornamento*. In the same vein,
it is striking that, in express contrast to the timidity and
conspiratorial obsessiveness of the present, Afghani, Abduh and many other prominent Muslim and Christian
figures of the *nahda* were extremely interested in Western
freemasonry, which they admired for its rationalist com-
mitment.

The *nahda* was a very wide-ranging phenomenon – a
time of regeneration and a beacon of progress – so the fact
that its nationalist dreams were thwarted could never be
grounds to consign it to oblivion. In any case, it lived on
after its supposed failure. Despite the irruption of colonialism which saw the waning Ottoman Empire shared
out among the European imperial powers, regardless of
Arab aspirations to independence, the spirit of the *nahda*
continued to inspire Arab struggles for emancipation.

V

THE ARAB MALAISE IS NOT THE RESULT OF MODERNITY BUT OF MODERNITY'S COLLAPSE

IF THE *NAHDA* had been an isolated historical phenomenon, without sequel, one might be justified in denying it any exemplary value. But it was nothing of the sort. As a historical moment and expression of nationalism, the *nahda* was undoubtedly over by the end of the First World War, but it lived on as an attitude and an outlook on the world. Despite the radical political breakdown of the fall of the Ottoman Empire and the rise of Western – French and British – domination in the Levant (with its apotheosis in Arab Africa), there was no noticeable discontinuity between the culture of the *nahda* and that of the 'short twentieth century'. If there was a radical change, then it came in the last two decades of that century.

Arab modernity, in other words, was not confined to a few decades of the nineteenth century. This is true as much for the history of ideas and cultural creation as it is for social history.

If literature is anything to go by, continuity was such
that public opinion readily confuses Arab cultural figures
of the first half of the twentieth century with the pioneers
of the *nahda*. The literary effervescence between the wars
picked up the spirit of renaissance; the 1920s in fact are
often depicted as the *tajdid*, the renewal. A publishing
boom as sustained as that of the height of the *nahda*
revealed   prose writers and, for the first time, poets
engaged in passionate exploration of new forms that both
enriched and remodelled Arabic, and kept it in tune with
the universal. The great writers of the time were citizens of
the world: the Egyptians Taha Hussein, a French-educated
confirmed secularist; Tawfiq al-Hakim, inseparable from
his beret, his badge of modernity; Ahmed Shawqi, 'prince
of poets' and poet of princes, the bard who sang of Rome,
Ancient Greece, Arab Andalusia and Egypt and Syria's
struggle for independence; the Lebanese Amin Rihani,
international globe-trotter, with one foot in America and
the other in his village, and open agnostic, which did not
stop Abdel Aziz, the future king and founder of devout
Saudi Arabia, making him a trusted friend.[21]

Rihani's travel writing reflected the new spirit. Arab
novels and short stories moved away from historical
fiction to realism and novels of manners, a shift in which
the new journalism played a part. But poetry was undoubtedly the most vivid expression of renewal: whereas
before a Parnassian, or even downright pompous, classi-
cism dominated, now a Baudelairean school, occasionally
with overtones of Apollinaire, began to emerge.

Amid this intellectual excitement, nationalist aspirations seem initially to have been relegated to the background, although they were apparent in certain works –
notably Ahmad Shawqi's poetry – and in the vogue for
trips to Andalusia. But Arab nationalism was not long in
making a comeback. It may have been anti-European
from now on, due to the frustrations surrounding the
settling of the Eastern Question, but it was no less a
product, in its content and all its variants, of the history of
European thought. All the thinkers behind its ideology
came from the Western school: Sati al-Husri, unquestionably the founding father of twentieth-century Arab
nationalism, and his youngest son, Michel Aflaq, who
created the Baath party after his return from the Sor-
bonne; Constantine Zurayq and Edmond Rabbath.[22] It
did not matter which nationalisms they promoted: the
pan-Syrianism of Antoun Saadeh, which exercised a
powerful appeal in Lebanon and Syria – and among
the Palestinians after 1948 – was inspired by German
nationalism, racialism included, while the hazy ideological
constructions of 'partial' nationalisms, like the Egyptian-
ism of Ahmad Lotfi al-Sayyed or the Phoenicianist
Lebanesism, drew on the liberal tradition.[23]

Between the wars modernization meant westernization
more than ever, and once again, people made their
reservations felt. Sometimes dramatically, like the religious establishment's campaigns in Egypt against Sheikh
Ali Abdel Razek's book on Islam and the foundations of
power, written in response to the abolition of the Ottoman

Caliphate in 1924, or against Taha Hussein's reinterpreta-
tion of the history of Arab poetry. These essentially
isolated campaigns were overshadowed by the founding
of the Muslim Brotherhood by Hassan al-Banna,[24] a
young man disgusted by the changes in Egyptian life,
which would come to exemplify a lasting resistance to the
westernization of daily life and culture. This was the first
statement of political Islam in the twentieth century, but it
would nonetheless be a long time before that became the
dominant ideology. So long as Western-style modernity
refrained from attacking the sacred head-on, it would
continue to prevail for several decades, as one can see
from the 1950s, the third era of renewal.

Paradoxically this age was ushered in by further
frustration and disappointment in the West, as it propped
up the new state of Israel on the ruins of Palestine. But
there was no related break with Western ways of thinking. The fact that the West was split between an im-
perialist 'free world' and socialism, the 'standard-bearer of
national liberation', certainly contributed. The influence
of socialist ideas shows that Arab thought was not tempted
to pull back from the universal. If Palestine's *nakba*, the
'catastrophe' of the declaration of the state of Israel, had
an effect, it was to introduce a sense of anguish to Arab
culture – a commodity European culture was also dis-
pensing at the time. Existential novels were being written
in Arabic by the mid-1950s, and when the revolution in
Arab poetry gathered steam at the start of the following
decade, having cast off the constrictions of traditional

prosody, Rimbaud took his place alongside Mutanabbi as the young poets' role model.[25]

Military coups d'état began to exacerbate the democratic deficit in a number of Arab countries, but in Cairo, Baghdad and Damascus – not to mention Beirut, the free zone of Arab culture – intellectual debate remained the daily bread of literary circles that, as result of the spread of modern education, were constantly growing. Contemporary poetry, despite a challenging pursuit of innovation, found a large audience. Each of Nizar Qabbani's collections sold in the thousands and although he may not have been the most adventurous in literary terms, the success of his erotic lyricism in praise of women – of liberated women, what's more – showed modernism's reach.[26] This was the moment Arab women started to promote their own revolution through their writings. Social conservatism began to yield to the mood of the time, with its halo of promise hovering over the struggle for national liberation.

Even the fresh Arab defeat of 1967 did not dampen the cultural effervescence. It was if anything a stimulus, hastening the adoption and adaptation of the counter-cultural thinking then prevalent in the world. All the variants of socialism were expressed, at least in book form. The religious establishment at times managed to impose its views – for example by banning the Syrian author Sadek Jalal al-Azm's *Critique of Religious Thought* in Beirut, as it had done before 1967 with Naguib Mahfouz's novel in Cairo – but it was secular, if not secularist, thought that determined cultural life and continued to do so virtually until the end of the 1970s – or even until the annihilation of Beirut after the Israeli siege in the summer of 1982. Certain authors think that this marked the real end of the adventure of the *nahda*, understood in its broadest historical sense. There's no doubt that, up until that moment, the spirit of renaissance had been a constant presence in the Arab world.

Arab cultural modernity in the twentieth century was probably even more far-reaching than during the nineteenth-century renaissance, since it went beyond the written word. Other forms of cultural creation presented themselves, different ways in which Arab artistic expression could reflect its time – in the visual arts, theatre, music and in particular the cinema.

Towards the end of the nineteenth century a taste for painting developed among the social elites of Arab cities most exposed to European influences; interior design began to incorporate reproductions of famous works of European painting; individuals responded to what they would later acknowledge as artistic vocations. But painting only ceased to be a marginal, isolated pursuit after the First World War; it became an art, even a profession. The Islamic injunction on representation was discarded without argument – without even debate – and a genuine visual-arts movement sprung up in several Arab cities. Of course there was still a big difference between what was happening in Europe, where cubism, and then surrealism, spelled the end of traditional figuration, and what was happening in the Arab world, where a belated and tentative form of impressionism was the only exception to realist portraiture. The two worlds came together after the Second World War. Progressing by leaps and bounds, artists in Egypt, Iraq, Syria, Lebanon and, soon afterwards, North Africa worked their way through the entire history of painting and sculpture in less than two decades, so that they were ready to embrace abstraction when its moment came.

Painting's audience naturally remained limited compared with that of another art form that developed at the same time: the theatre. Introduced in the middle of the nineteenth century by the Beiruti Maroun Naccache[27] and encouraged in certain schools, it found its chosen ground in Egypt in the twentieth century where comedy, particularly a kitsch version of vaudeville, became enormously popular. After Molière, who Naccache adapted, plays by Feydeau and Labiche were Egyptianized; Rostand's works followed with Fatima Rushdie, the 'Sarah Bernhardt of the East', immortalizing L'Aiglon. Egyptian authors also wrote their own plays, encouraged by the demand that extended beyond Egypt as Cairo's companies toured other Arab cities. Yet it was not until the 1960s that the theatre developed outside Egypt, first in Iraq, Syria and Lebanon, and then in Morocco, Algeria and Tunisia. In all these countries the theatre was seen as a vehicle for ideas. Local experiments in vaudeville were successful, but theatre companies chiefly wanted to comment on society and so initially drew on the contemporary Western repertoire, particularly Brecht. It was not long, however, before local playwrights established themselves.

Not so political in the main, but extremely popular, Arabic song was also, despite appearances, part of this process of westernization. Until the end of the twentieth century, the songs thankfully never shrunk anywhere near the Western three-minute standard, even though 45s did in practice lead to some cutting. But even the *qasida*, the long poem that proved the perfect vehicle for Om Kulthum's unique voice,[28] shows the extent of Western influence. The lyrics are in the tradition of the revitalized – although not yet revolutionized – poetry of the 1920s and 1930s, and although the music kept the quarter tone, Sayyed Darwish[29] brought in a completely new orchestration. Violin and cello became the backbone of a new Arab music until the advent of the electric guitar, adopted by – who else – Om Kulthum at the start of 1970s.

But of all the arts, the cinema best illustrates the Arabs' embrace of modernity. Once again Egypt was the driving force, accounting for three-quarters – maybe more – of Arab film production. Its success, and the demand for its films throughout the Arab world, made it a transnational Arab phenomenon.

After the Italian community in Egypt introduced filmmaking in the 1920s, the growth of Egyptian cinema coincided with the talkies, which crucially opened up the possibility of musicals, one of the motors of the industry's success. Then the Misr Studios opened in 1935 under the aegis of the banker Talaat Harb, a model nationalist capitalist, and despite their ups and downs, were to make Cairo the third capital of the world's film industry, after Hollywood and Bombay but ahead of Italy's Cinecittà.

Besides the cult of entertainment that led the Egyptian and Arab public in general to worship the stars of the big screen – in particular its singers – the cinema also showed the excitement Middle Eastern societies felt at how their daily life and symbolic representations were changing. Often backed up by great writers who had no qualms about seeing their novels turned into films or who wrote the scripts themselves, Egyptian directors rendered modernity in black and white, then Technicolor – a modernity that was transfiguring the image of women, who, after the spectacular taboo-breaking of Hoda Shaarawi, the women's rights activist who was first to take off her veil in public at Cairo station in 1922, controlled their appearances if not their bodies.[30] Idealized on a monumental scale by the posters in the street, women underwent a startling change of public image: previously recluses, they were now the crowds' idols. Other women in the wings made no less of a contribution to modernization – if there were no female directors, there were certainly influential female producers.

This was such a radical transformation that, despite vicissitudes, its effects will never be cancelled out, either by the return of a puritanism which since the 1980s has driven former romantic heroines of the silver screen to veil themselves, or by feminist critiques of the female body being turned into a sex object. Incidentally there is nothing specifically Arab about its films' sexualization of movie stars, as Cairo frequently copies Hollywood – nor anything specifically female either, since men are just as much sex objects.

The cinema embraced modernity not only through its symbolism but also in its business logic, drawing on Egyptian financiers and technicians and the Syrian and Lebanese communities equally. It wasn't affected by the switch from economic liberalism to state capitalism either. Although Nasser's Egypt sought to distance itself from the cosmopolitanism of Alexandria and Khedival Cairo, it chose not to alienate the cinema. It even supported the industry, using it to add some big-screen magic to its revolutionary symbolism. As with the rest of the Egyptian economy, the crisis came after the end of Nasserism, when the problems of ultraliberalism meshed with those of state bureaucracy. It must also be said that this coincided with the Arab identity crisis, fuelled by the rise of political Islam.

Given the popular, transnational success of Egyptian cinema, one obviously cannot claim to believe, as one perhaps might with other forms of artistic expression, that cultural modernity was the prerogative of a tiny elite. Particularly since, after the so-called 'white telephones' phase of luxurious fantasy, films portrayed the sort of men and women you could see on any street in Cairo, Baghdad or Damascus (looking slightly less glamorous, no doubt).

In most Arab cities, a new standard of modernity was set in daily life. The battle of the veil, after Hoda Shaarawi's declaration of independence and Atatürk's programme in Turkey had dominated the 1920s, ended in victory for 'deveiling'. Not wearing the veil was an individual decision in Egypt, rather than an authoritarian government ruling like in Turkey, and this was what made it a real revolution that gradually spread to other countries until the veil had become sufficiently rare in the 1960s to make its appearance noteworthy. It is true that women didn't have the same freedom of appearance throughout the Arab world and legislation took time to catch up – although Syrian women got the vote before the French. Social conservatism, although systematically pushed back, continued to predominate, but it was generally no more marked than in Franco's Spain or Greece before the tourism boom.

The Arab world did not adapt to modernity in a uniform way. In North Africa, colonialism's demarcation between the European city and the Arab city inhibited the adoption of any of 'the Whites'' behavioural norms. But independence saw the same changes there in daily life as in Egypt and the Levant. The profound exception was the Arabian peninsula, which had been on the fringes of Arab culture for centuries. When modernity belatedly burst onto the scene in those countries, it was purely technological. Women remained secluded; the veil didn't give an inch. The opposite was in fact the case: it was in large measure the fact of Saudis and Kuwaitis travelling the

world in national dress, with the women covered from
head to toe in black *abaya*, that made the veil commonplace again and paved the way for societies to regress to a
world before Hoda Shaarawi. This rejection of modernity
in turn coincided with the onset of the Arab malaise.

Although an *idée fixe* would have it so, it was not Arab
nationalism that arrested the development of modernity.
As I have already shown, the ideological Arabism that
followed the irruption of colonialism was itself a product
of the encounter with Europe. What's more, in practice,
especially in the Levant, this ideology was marked by a
cultural Jacobinism inherited from the French Revolution,
and imperial culture was abandoned in the name of the
nation-state, despite there being no actual nation-state to
step into the breach.

The nationalist promotion of Arabic to the exclusion of
all other languages has no doubt fanned hostility towards
other cultures, yet it too is a product of European modernity.
The linguistic nationalism of the Arabist theoreticians
derives largely from their reading of Fichte. Other European influences – sometimes several at once – are discernible in the different nationalisms. The Baath party, for
instance, whose military leaders took the marginalization of
foreign languages to its furthest extreme in Syria, was the
product of an ideological synthesis that, at least initially,
placed a great deal of emphasis on French personalism.

It may have taken a more radical turn after the Arab
defeat in Palestine in 1948, but Arabism continued to be

universalist: internationally, in its South–South solidarity and role in the Third World and non-alignment, and domestically in its drive towards economic modernization that implemented European models, although in authoritarian forms. Despite breaking with liberal parliamentarianism, which it has to be said was relatively ineffective, Arab politics continued to use imported terms, such as 'the masses', 'revolution' and 'socialism'.

Of course it would be impossible to paint an idyllic picture of this era, if only because the absence of democracy and the excesses of state control drained the Arab world of all initiative and paved the way for the present chaos. Nonetheless, Arabs did regain an international presence during this brief period. Nasser's Egypt became one of the pillars of Africa and the Third World; Algeria was a beacon for the oppressed; Bourguiba's Tunisia pushed through secularism; and although they didn't achieve this degree of political will, many other Arab societies adapted with no moral dilemmas to the secularization of daily life, a process dramatized in cinema and literature in a way that would be inconceivable now.

So it is clear that the lesson of Arab history cannot be that Arabs are powerless to regain the power and status they once possessed. If Arabs could re-enter universal history forty years ago, then nothing should stop them being reconciled with the spirit of synthesis – cultural and political – that has been the hallmark of their long history when they emerge from their malaise and cease to be the centre of a world in crisis.

VI

THE ARABS' MALAISE IS MORE
A FUNCTION OF THEIR GEOGRAPHY
THAN THEIR HISTORY

Are the Arabs the centre of the world? Setting aside Arab discourse, the part they have played in international affairs for over half a century suggests one shouldn't dismiss such a seemingly presumptuous question too hastily.

The Palestinian question and the Arab–Israeli conflict, virtually uninterrupted since the end of the Second World War; the Suez crisis and its knock-on effects; the Algerian war; more recently, the long chapter of the Lebanese war; the upheavals in Iraq, from the Iran war to the invasion of Kuwait and the American occupation; the convulsions of Islamism in Egypt and Algeria; September 11's repercussions in the Arabian peninsula, to mention only the most striking episodes – so much has happened that has focused the attention of the world's media and governments on the Arab world. Editors may cite the dramatic nature of events or their significance in terms of international affairs as justification for their front pages, but this prominence equally emphasizes the all-too-often-forgotten factor of geography.

To understand the history of the Arab world, one must inevitably take account of its geography, particularly because the region is atypical from a geographical point of view. Straddling two continents, not all its terrestrial borders are natural; moreover, its identity lies primarily in its shared history and a deep seam of shared culture (however diversified its expressions have been, and continue to be). Both these elements explain the existence of a regional organization defined by linguistic identity, the League of Arab States, and the prevailing use of a voluntarist term, the Arab 'homeland', for the region. Atypical though it may be, however, this geography does have a number of features that have shaped contemporary Arab history.

The first and unquestionably foremost of these is its position in the heart of the Old World, facing Europe. It is almost a truism to say that their region's proximity to Europe has had the most implications for the Arabs. There's no need here to retrace the long history it has engendered: from the conquest of Andalusia and Sicily to the colonization of Algeria, by way of the crusades and the imperial division of the Levant after the collapse of the Ottoman Empire. Suffice to say that the Arab world is the only part of the colonial world to have confronted Europe in the pre-colonial era and to have dominated the encounter for long stretches. This alone explains why the European view of Arabs is rarely neutral, while fuelling

Arabs' resentment at no longer being the power they were.

Once Europe had established itself as a global power and was bent on expanding overseas, the Arab world by its very proximity was fated to become Europe's stepping stone. Neither the crossing of the Atlantic, nor the circumnavigation of Africa, courtesy of Vasco de Gama's Arab navigators, reduced the Mediterranean's significance. In fact, with the expansion of European trade that followed the end of the Napoleonic wars, control of the Mediterranean, now ascendant Europe's *mare nostrum*, once again became a major prize. At stake were the Ottoman markets, heavily targeted by British and French manufacturers, and above all European imperial ambitions. North Africa commanded the western gateway of the Mediterranean, while Egypt held the key to the east both the land route to India and the second sea route that opened up with the Suez Canal.

While the geographic factor may not completely explain the complexity of the Eastern Question, one can still see its influence at some of the most significant moments in the region's history. Even before the Suez Canal was built, the British Empire had been alarmed by the rise of Muhammad Ali, ally of the July Monarchy,[31] and had gone to the aid of the future Sick Man of Europe with Austria and Russia (despite the fact that the latter had designated the Ottoman Empire its 'hereditary enemy'). France then had to join them to preserve the European alliance, at which point the first idea of a Jewish state or, more specifically, a Jewish kingdom, was mooted. There were no Jewish founding fathers at this stage, only English Protestants whose rationale, purely strategic, was the potential benefit to Great Britain in having a buffer zone between Egypt and Syria under its control.

This plan had no immediate consequences; the other British project of the time, concerning India, was more concrete. In 1839, Great Britain took possession of the port of Aden at the mouth of the Red Sea and established the town and hinterland as a colony – the future South Yemen, which became a Marxist-Leninist state in 1968. The issue of the security of the Indies route also entailed control of the Persian Gulf, a bolt-hole for pirates plying the Indian Ocean. Rather than direct rule, the British navy opted for the protectorate system, initially imposing a treaty on the sheikhs of the region, which turned the Pirate coast into the Truce coast, now the United Arab Emirates. The same approach was used in 1899 with the sheikh of the little town of Kuwait – even though Ottoman rule was more overt there in the form of the Governor of Bassora – and the Sultanate of Mascate.

In the meantime the British hadn't forgotten Egypt. Despite the waning of Egyptian ambitions after Muhammad Ali's death, geography remained decisive. Failing to block the construction of the Suez Canal, London decided to take control of it once it was built, first economically, by 'redeeming' the debt-crippled Khedive Ismail's shares in the Universal Company, and then strategically, by using the same debts as grounds to impose a protectorate, which was to last three-quarters of a century.

An identical geopolitical logic dictated the division of Ottoman spoils in the context of the Great War. The Levant was obviously a target in itself, for France as much as for Great Britain. Yet it was the part it played in their imperial strategies that prompted the two great powers, allies and rivals by turns, to consider it a major prize. At stake for Great Britain was the security of the Suez Canal, which in turn guaranteed British command of the Indies. London was consequently prepared to go to any lengths to control Palestine, including backing a new version of the plan for a Jewish state formulated by the nascent Zionist movement. Conversely, the sense Britain had after the Second World War that it would have to give up India influenced its decision not to make a stand to keep Palestine when its former Zionist allies turned against it. As for France, while possession of 'French Syria' – Syria and Lebanon combined – was certainly in the interests of Lyons's and Marseilles's business circles, its real attraction was that of ensuring France's continued colonial domination of North Africa, culturally rather than geographically. This explains why France, after having to renounce Palestine, was anxious to divide Syria, and then stubbornly insisted on keeping it on, despite the cost. According to an idea already current at the start of the century among activists of the Committee of French Asia, but only explicitly formulated between the wars by the Orientalist Robert Montagne, whoever controlled the

Levant, home of the nascent Arab nationalism, would
control the Maghreb and the new air route to Indochina.

Anyone can of course choose to skip this entire history of
domination and simply say that Arabs, unable to see the
real benefits, have always looked the modernizing gift
horse of the West in the mouth. But, apart from disregarding how much acculturation has gone on for the last
century and a half, such a view obscures how beleaguered
the Arabs have been: first by having to defend themselves
against colonial powers, then by having to liberate
themselves from colonial supremacy. You can put a
number on the human cost of the Algerian war, just as
you can count the thousands of Egyptian peasants who
died building the Suez Canal. But how can you calculate
the economic and political price of the tension that grips
people searching for their place in the sun, when they
come up against the obstacle of daily foreign domination?
How can you say how much energy has been diverted
away from development by the colonizer's presence? How
can you quantify what the social sphere has lost to the
cause of political mobilization? How can you express the
sacrifice the Individual has to make in the People's
debilitating struggle?
    The Arab world is clearly not the only region that has
been forced to fall behind in its development because its
liberation struggle took priority (how could it not?). But of
the entire colonial world, only the Arabs have been
exposed throughout the twentieth century – and into

the twenty-first – to the stratagems of power that their geography seems permanently to invite. The end of the colonial era did not signify an end to the imperial threat for them. Only a few Arab states won independence – of a largely nominal sort – and as colonial domination waned, the setting-up of a foreign state that presented itself as the West's intermediary caught the Arabs off guard.

This is the real meaning, and certainly the real effect, of Palestine's *nakba*. It was not simply a catastrophe because the defeat of the Palestinians and five Arab armies at the hands of the Zionist Haganah, or Tsahal as it was renamed,[32] was seen as a humiliation – the Arabs at the time not knowing that the Haganah was larger, and of course better equipped, than all their troops put together; nor because in emptying Palestine of its Arabness and making refugees of its people, the foundation of the state of Israel interrupted the human, political and cultural continuity of the Levant. It was a catastrophe above all because it signified to the Arabs – at least to those of the Levant – that foreign rule, which seemed to be on its way out after the Second World War, was there to stay and that they were as helpless to confront it as they had been at the end of the First World War. This was made to seem even more damning when the victorious state of Israel in turn refused to compromise on the partition plan which the Arabs belatedly said they were ready to accept after the Conference of Lausanne. Revolving around this permanent source of crisis, the entire political life of the Middle East was marked by the unbalance of power between Israel and the Arab states from then on and, in an extremely revealing way, Iraq, one of the potential leaders of the Arab world, ended up being marginalized. Geographically removed from the conflict, it would not play a major role again in Arab affairs until another threat emerged, much later, on its eastern flank.

Crushing though it was, the *nakba* did not prevent a reaction in Arab countries. A series of military coups d'état followed: liberal parliamentarianism was shelved, except in Lebanon, and, unable to redress the power imbalance with Israel, the new regimes wasted no time in putting their societies behind bars. One can obviously lament this, and reject the argument that such political authoritarianism is necessary in times of confrontation with foreign hegemony. But if one considers history without the anachronism of hindsight, isn't it possible to understand that Arab societies as a whole, not just their ruling generals, wanted a moral and military rearmament? This question seems all the more legitimate because the Arab reaction wasn't purely militarist, as Nasser shows. That extraordinary chapter saw Egypt put an end to Great Britain's imperial hegemony for good, become an international political player at the forefront of the Third World and Non-Alignment movement, and make undeniable domestic progress, first of all in education, then in development and social democracy.

In the end, the Nasserite adventure no doubt failed. But here again, how can one disregard the debilitating effects of the conflict with Israel, and, perhaps even more significant, the role this conflict played in the strategies of the world powers? First, Egypt's two former colonial rulers, Great Britain and France, band together in 1956 to ask Israel to give them an opportunity for revenge against Nasser. Then the new American superpower sets up 1967's nasty surprise with a skilful campaign of diplomatic disinformation, and uses the paralysing effects of the Arabs' defeat to advance its pawns in the Great Game of the Cold War and impose a *Pax Americana* in Israel and the Middle East - which, it transpires, will be an indefinitely prolonged form of crisis management.

The Arab–Israeli conflict shows that the end of the colonial era did not render obsolete the geopolitical calculations that had determined the history of the Arab world until then. The Mediterranean, along with the Persian Gulf, continued to focus the attention of the world powers on the region – initially in the context of the Cold War, where the Mediterranean played a fundamental role in NATO strategy. The Great Game staple of the Russian push towards warm seas was reinvented in the context of the confrontation between the two blocs, and the obsession with containment thereby transferred to the Middle East, with incongruous effects. The Cold War-influenced policies of the West – America, Britain and France – drove first Nasser's Egypt, then Syria, and then Iraq to turn to the USSR, a state of affairs that only seemed to reinforce the 'free world's' imperial designs on the Middle East. These had begun to take on a new urgency at the end of the 1970s, when the Soviet invasion of Afghanistan revived the fear of the Russian push south and, combined with the repercussions of the Iranian revolution, made control of the Arab world's eastern flank an absolute necessity for the West.

In the meantime the realities of geography had been supplemented by those of geology. The Arab world may have had its place in imperial policy before the discovery of its reserves of hydrocarbons – and even before oil's economic utility became paramount – but oil entrenched power's strategies. Prospected but not yet exploited, Mosul's oil was already at the heart of British and French negotiations at the end of the First World War; by rejecting the first version of the Sykes–Picot agreement, the latter retained their interests in it. Oil also anticipated the new hegemony of the United States in the Middle East. In the 1930s, the major American oil companies began doling out sinecures to cement their alliance with the founder of Saudi Arabia, King Abdel Aziz; the relationship was sanctioned by the meeting on Roosevelt's yacht in the middle of the Second World War.

Oil will never cease to cloud people's minds. Whatever the conditions in which it is produced, it will remain essential to the economies of the industrialized countries. Neither the development of other sources of energy since the historic readjustment of prices in 1973, nor the stockpiling of substantial reserves in the West has shown any sign of sidelining the question of the oilfields' security – quite apart from the fact that the oil-producing countries also contain a wealth of raw materials, and have constituted a massive export market for the West since the 1973 boom.

The geography of oil wealth has also had a devastating effect on the internal balance of the Arab world. By an extraordinary quirk of nature, the main hydrocarbon deposits are in countries that have remained on the fringes of Arab history for centuries, and that have hence experienced an atypical political and cultural development. The two exceptions in this are Iraq and Algeria, and, whatever the follies committed in both countries, their oil wealth is qualified by their demographic size. The main reason the countries of the Arabian peninsula, and Libya, have become so immensely rich is that their wealth hasn't had to be shared out between a large population – or at any rate hasn't been. In Saudi Arabia poverty has started coming to light in the past few years that had previously seemed utterly inconceivable. The manna of oil has given the governing elites of these countries the ability to intervene in inter-Arab relations, and so oil has ensured that the entire Arab world can share the backwardness of the Arabian peninsula.

This is the other consequence of geography. While Saudi Arabia may have made considerable technical progress, it has profoundly set back the Hijaz region to the west of the peninsula: the birthplace of Islam, this used to be the least isolated, least culturally backward part of the country, in tandem with Syria for centuries. Above all, though, Saudi Arabia has set back the entire Arab world, the most distressing proofs of which are the invisible faces of women which it has re-exported virtually everywhere.

VII

THE WORST ASPECT OF THE ARABS' MALAISE IS THEIR REFUSAL TO EMERGE FROM IT, BUT, IF HAPPINESS IS NOT IN SIGHT, SOME FORM OF EQUILIBRIUM AT LEAST IS POSSIBLE

SOME PEOPLE ARE driven to despair by the Arab malaise. They believe that the Arabs are so profoundly trapped that they will never be able to break free and, in so believing, they only make the deadlock worse. This is the extreme variant of modernism, propounded by liberals, disappointed nationalists and former activists of the left alike. Decline, according to this way of thinking, is so widespread that it damns the very notion of a renaissance: the *nahda* did not just end in failure, but it was also by its very nature a historical anomaly, an impossibility right from the outset. Worse still, all attempts to free the Arabs from their predicament, particularly nationalism, are considered to have only made the problem worse. Some of these disappointed souls go so far as to internalize the culturalist distinctions that legitimize imperial domination. Their most affirmative thesis, echoing the American neoconservatives, is that change and democracy can only come from such domination, not realizing that all this will achieve is to aggravate frustrations, exacerbate victimhood and the culture of death, and thereby perpetuate the Arab malaise. For, if they are to overcome their malaise, the Arabs have no choice but to do it themselves.

Then there are those people for whom things are never better than when everything's wrong. Obviously these are the Islamist jihadists who, as good messianists, see the Arab malaise just as a bad moment to be got through – well, not as bad as all that actually, since it can be a way to gain paradise and the forty *houris* while waiting for that strange revolution which, unlike its Marxist original, is not seen as a leap into the future, but as a return to an original purity lost in the mists of time.

As a system of thought, jihadist Islamism is far from being the dominant ideology it is often portrayed as in the Western media. Yet it is powerful, no doubt because it is the only ideology that seems to offer relief from the victim status the Arabs delight in claiming (a status that in fact Islamism, jihadist or otherwise, is only too happy to confirm).

Arab victimhood goes beyond the 'Why do they hate us?' question, which Arabs would be as entitled to ask as the Americans were on the morning of September 11. Inflamed by the West's attitude to the Palestinian question, it has incorporated other elements, notably the feeling of powerlessness and also a certain crime-novel vision of history.

The cult of the victim claims that Arabs are the West's primary target, totally disregarding the other peoples of the world, and world history in general. No mention is made of Africa and its systematic pillaging; of the Americas and the genocide of the pre-Columbian populations, perpetuated in the continued marginalization of their cultures, of Indochina and its decimated generations . . .

Of course I am not denying what we have presupposed, that the Arabs have nothing that might compensate them for their misfortune, and that the Arab world is the only region on earth where the West has continually acted as if it were the master – and still does today, either directly or through Israel. But this doesn't change the fact that recognizing the threat to the Arab world is not the same as condoning Arab victimhood. None of the major figures of the renaissance showed any signs of indulging such a cult, nor the ideologues or practitioners of nationalism. Victims *par excellence*, the Palestinians avoided it in the past, and continue in a very large degree to do so, even if their situation fosters a propensity among those who helplessly look on to claim such a status.

Victimhood is the price of the defeat of the universal, rather than a product of the status quo, and its cult, served by the Arab media, in particular the much-lionized Al-Jazeera, has only been able to grow because the ideology of the moment preaches a refusal of the universal. Ideology is in fact a very grand word for the current amalgam of the fossilized remains of Arab nationalism, which, because of their age, have cut themselves off from their original, universalist sources of inspiration, and an 'Islamic nationalism' that explicitly sets out to differentiate itself from the universal, if not supplant it. Such a nationalist mishmash is not new. It was around at the end of the nineteenth century, propounded notably by Afghani. The only difference is that Afghani was a reformer of Islam, with a perfect knowledge of, and uninhibited dealings with, Western thought. The same cannot be said of his present-day successors, who abhor nothing so much as talk of religious reform.

Islamic nationalism isn't just a synonym for jihadism. It is defensive in essence, whereas jihadism can in certain lights see itself as a new conquest of the world. But the distinction between the two is nonetheless a tenuous one, and there can be no doubt that Islamic nationalism prepares the ground for jihadism. For while it may not deny the Arab malaise, as jihadism does, it nonetheless predisposes those who complain of the malaise to wallow in it, so much so that they will only replace it with something similar: the culture of death which the union of fossilized Arab nationalism and political Islam calls resistance.

There is undoubtedly an inherent explanation of the culture of death – not that it is an invariant of Islam or an essence of Arabness, but rather that, as a spectacle of endless bloodshed, it instils a self-perpetuating logic of blood for blood. If there can be no victory, then at least there can be the consolation of bloodletting – others' blood, obviously, but ours as well.

This logic may not be an invariant of Islam, but the fact remains that a religious vision of the world is at work here, even a religious vision in the sense of a system of cruelty, as Nietzsche put it. It goes without saying that this has nothing to do with the idea of sacrifice. Sacrifice has been at the root of all human conflict since the dawn of history, for the Arabs as much as anyone else, and this is the real meaning of *jihad* in the martial sense (there are also peaceful forms of *jihad*). In the twentieth century, the Palestinian fighters called themselves *fedayeen*, those ready to sacrifice their lives, like the Egyptian nationalists before them who fought the British at Suez. But in the new jihadism, death has ceased to be a potential, or even probable, price to be paid. Death has become the indispensable means to a desired end, if not an actual end in itself.

This vision of martial *jihad* incarnated in the figure of the *istishhadi*, the one who seeks martyrdom (the kamikaze, in other words), has no real antecedent in Arab–Muslim culture apart from the – non-Arab – sect of the Assassins. In the modern era, one has to wait until the Iranian revolution for its return. Shia at first, it emerged on the frontline of the Iraq–Iran war, where unbroken waves of volunteers checked the advance of the Iraqi armoured divisions before launching themselves against the Iraqi lines at the start of 1982. It appeared next in Lebanon in the form of individual suicide attacks against Western interests and the Israeli occupying forces. It should be noted that this extreme method may have been effective against the Americans, but traditional guerrilla tactics — ambushes, explosions and so on — were more decisive against the Israelis. Nonetheless other groups, some of them secular, adopted it as a model. Hezbollah gave it up when it became the only method of resistance, but kept the symbolism of blood and the totem of the *istishhadi* — a symbolism that it reinforces through the observance of Ashura. Originating in Iranian Shiism before passing to Lebanon and now Iraq, the rituals of this festival of redemptive suffering resemble certain bloody celebrations of Good Friday, in Spain for instance or the Philippines.

In principle, an insurmountable obstacle divides the Shia and the Sunni jihadists. Radical Sunni Islamism, as the doctrinal statements that have been coming out of Iraq show, holds Shia to be heretics and *rafida*, people who reject the true faith. Sunni Qur'anic literalism clearly also has its intellectual origins in South Asian Islam, notably the thought of Mawdudi, which, through the conduit of the Egyptian Sayyid Qutb, has permeated its *takfiri*, or apostatizing, strain.[33] None of this matters, however. The martyrdom seekers first appeared in Shia circles, with the *shahids* recording their last testaments on video (the price of modernity). Furthermore, of the two Palestinian groups that have practised suicide bombing, one, Islamic Jihad, is reputed to be close to Iran, while the other, Hamas, although an offshoot of the Muslim Brotherhood, is on very good terms with Lebanese Hezbollah.

The proliferation of the culture of death and the

evening-out of differences between Shias and Sunnis cannot be explained solely by the Islamization of the fight against Israel. Over and above actual events, the media, especially Al-Jazeera, has played a key role in this process, peddling a lowest-common-denominator mix of Arab nationalism and Islamic nationalism. It was doing this before September 11, defending means, justifying ends, claiming Arab victimhood. The Arab public has been systematically primed to accept the thesis of a 'clash of civilizations'.

Nonetheless, we must be able to continue rebutting Huntingdon and remembering Lévi-Strauss. If we could address the protagonists of the 'war against terror' or the 'jihad against the crusaders' in academic terms, that ought surely to be the watchword of a new universalism.

Nothing is harder than rebutting Huntingdon at a time when people are doing their utmost to cultivate difference. On the one hand, politicians and commentators constantly invoke an Eastern essentialism, even if, after long tirades opposing 'us' and 'them', they see fit to stress that Arabs and Muslims should not all be lumped in with the terrorists. On the other, there is a tendency to qualify, or even justify, the horrors of New York in terms of the evils of American politics, even if people are careful to preface their remarks with the disclaimer that the murder of innocent people goes against every precept of Islam.

We must not forget Lévi-Strauss: 'civilization', as he says, is not a category and hence cannot contain 'natural' hierarchies; and humanity is one, since it rests on a common anthropological foundation. In other words, it is as meaningless to talk of an 'attack on civilization' as it is to classify people according to their adherence to a faith, Muslim or otherwise. I should perhaps point out that supremacy isn't exclusively white. Some people in Muslim societies may be drawn to radical Islam for defensive reasons, because they feel under threat, but the rhetoric used by the warlords of radical Islamism is intentionally offensive. They justify their triumphalist proselytizing by defining the 'decadent' civilization of the Other as inferior.

So it is not just the West that needs to re-examine its stance. The Arab world in particular needs to make a profound effort to eradicate the ambiguities that encourage a logic of cultural confrontation. This means first putting victimhood into perspective. We must replace Arabs' customary assumption of victim status not by cultivating a logic of power or a spirit of revenge, but by recognizing the fact that, despite bringing defeats, the twentieth century has also brought benefits that can enable Arabs to participate in progress. Equally, we must reject the moral pragmatism lurking in the cult of the victim. If we cannot accept the powerful saying that the ends justify the means, then we can't let the victims do so either. We must not confuse terrorism with resistance, as the West confuses resistance with terrorism.

But, apart from the effects and means of confrontation, if the Arab world is to reject a clash of civilizations, then we must also give up a negative Arabocentrism (or Islamocentrism) which sees world history purely as a threat to us, and as a 'cultural', rather than political or military, threat. By the same token, we must renounce essentialist justifications of the sort that explain the silence surrounding the long affair of the Western hostages in Lebanon in the 1980s, or the indulgent attitudes towards the *fatwa* against Salman Rushdie. We must accept that democratic values are now part of humanity's shared heritage.

Such a re-examination could take place. The problem is that the elites that might push for it are caught between non-democratic regimes (frequently supported by the West, despite the 'democratic crusade' in the Middle East), on the one hand, and radical Islamism on the other. It goes without saying that the task would be easier if it was accompanied by another renaissance that had as many forms as it did inspirations, a renaissance that is still perfectly possible.

The despairing view of Arab thought and culture as permanently ensnared in conservativism and fanaticism has obscured several phenomena that could prepare a way out of the crisis. The first, which has been underway for the past two decades without its full extent becoming apparent, is the growth of a homogeneous and, at the same time, plural field of Arab culture. Despite the fragmentation of states and hence the market, and despite cultural borders patrolled by national censors, this field of

Arab culture is in many ways the most definitive expression of a cohesive Arabness at a time when all other attempts at integration – economical, political, pan-Arab and sub-regional – are deadlocked.

The phenomenon hasn't sprung fully formed out of nothing; the continuity of Arab culture is hardly new. If there is a novelty in the present variant, at least in terms of the contemporary period, it is the fact that there are so many centres of cultural production. During the nineteenth and the greater part of the twentieth century, cultural production was concentrated in the Levant, between the Nile valley and Mesopotamia. Cairo reigned supreme – in film, novels and music – with Beirut the challenger. What characterizes contemporary Arab culture is that creation and production are distributed among the majority of the Arab countries. Having come to independence late after a period of colonial rule that explicitly denied its Arabness, North Africa has been exceptionally quick to contribute. But the irruption of the Gulf States and the Arabian peninsula onto the scene, although they still lag behind, has been no less remarkable, considering that they have been cut off from Arab urbanity since Umayyad times.

It is clear, however, that this field is homogeneous in terms of the circulation of ideas and their expression, rather than their content. In this respect, although it is not fully aware it is doing so, Arab culture has begun to relearn how to integrate plurality into its unity of place and time, and stop thinking of difference as a source of division. The theorizing of otherness will probably always be inadequate as a condition of democracy; at best, it only concerns an elite. But that does not mean one cannot see it as a first step to accepting diversity.

Mirroring the enhanced circulation of ideas and cultural properties in the Arab world, despite substantial obstacles, is another, near parallel phenomenon: the Arab cultural field is beginning to be integrated into the mosaic of global culture. The emigration of large numbers of Arab creative artists to Europe after the destruction of Beirut produced a network of creative exchanges, both informal and structured, that have made Arab culture less marginalized in the world and more integrated in Europe. Cultural financing and co-production networks have been equally influential. They are a commonplace resource now, partly because of the number of Arab artists in Europe, and partly because of the availability of funding as a result of national and European political cooperation and NGO activism. People may often draw on them for reasons of convenience, or plain opportunism, but they have still produced a thematic convergence; issues that have crystallized elsewhere have spread through the field of Arab culture. Besides the arts, a good example of this process is the speed with which the question of gender has been taken up, entering the vocabularly as the neologism *jandara*. Of course there is a risk that such exchanges only produce an artificial veneer, especially if the convergence is restricted to an elite that is in touch with the outside world anyway. This increases the danger of a chauvinistic

popular reaction which can be manipulated, as several
poisonous controversies have recently shown: the affair of
Saad Eddin Ibrahim, for instance, who was tried and
sentenced in Egypt for receiving foreign financing,
although he was eventually cleared.[34]

In a similar vein, although for different motives,
economic actors in the global cultural market are beginning to take an interest in the Arab world, starting with its
music. Arabic music has been adopted by world music
later than its African counterpart, but Arabs are now
striving to become an integral part of the scene, and this
has led to a proliferation of subcultures, which are in
reality much more meaningful than the culture of the Arab
elite. Here too there has been resistance, negative press
reaction to certain videos and music programmes, for
instance, especially in the Arabian peninsula.

Another aspect of globalization, the revolution in
electronic media, is increasingly causing Arab culture
explicity to integrate the Other in its diversity. While
the internet may be the prerogative of a new, albeit
growing, elite, satellite channels, whatever their orienta-
tion, give the majority access to a visual and information
culture, which thereby situates the Arab world in a
composite global geography. This shows how, contrary
to a fearful vision of Arab identity, cultural globalization
could be Arab culture's great chance.

Surveying the panorama of contemporary Arab culture, its creativity and its networks for the circulation of
information, the Arab future should inspire greater opti-

mism. Naguib Mahfouz may have been the only Nobel Prize winner thus far, but half a dozen other writers deserve to follow in his footsteps, judging by the decisions of the Swedish Academy, and the Arab world can pride itself on being one of the few cultural spheres where poets not only sell on a large scale but are also at the forefront of world poetry.

But there's no talk of optimism. The Arab world, the Levant in particular, remains the prisoner of a political and social system that may allow diversity to express itself, but never allows it to translate into any change in the decision-making processes.

In this situation, it is obvious that the economic and political structures, blocked by internal and global balances of power, play a decisive role in perpetuating the deadlock. We cannot ignore social obstacles, but nor should we infer an anthropological impossibility from them. As we have seen, the history of Arab Islam belies any such view of Arab culture. The lack of interface between the culture of creation and the social culture is of much greater concern, and perhaps that is where we should seek solutions: in the galvanizing effect that new media can have on cultural development, and that culture in turn can have on durable economic development.

It is no doubt too ambitious to envisage an end to the cycle of malaise in the immediate future. Arab under-development has reached such proportions that one

cannot expect spirits to lift straight away; the persistence
of the West's hegemony, exacerbated by America's occupation of Iraq and Israel's ever-growing supremacy,
precludes a swift Arab awakening. But nothing, neither
foreign domination nor the economies' structural flaws –
let alone Arab cultural heritage – should prevent one
seeking the possibility of some form of equilibrium,
despite the terrible conditions at present.

This will require many things, not all of which depend
on the Arabs. But if we can't assemble them all, we can
still force destiny's hand by starting with what is most
urgent, what is indispensable to recovery: that we Arabs
abandon our fantasy of a matchless past and finally see our
real history, so that we can then be true to it.

NOTES

1 The Non-Alignment movement is an international organization of over 100 states which consider themselves not formally aligned with or against any major power bloc.
2 Muhammad Ali Pasha (CE c.1769–1849), viceroy of Egypt, and widely held to be the founder of modern Egypt.
3 *Makhzen*, literally 'warehouse', is a term for the governing elite in Morocco, often considered a barrier to democracy.
4 The secularist Habib Bourguiba (CE 1903–2000), first president of Tunisia (CE 1957–87), enacted pro-Western reforms during his presidency, promoting education and women's rights.
5 Houari Boumédienne (CE 1932–78), president of Algeria (CE 1965–78) initiated a programme of state driven industrialisation, natio nalizing the oil industry in 1971.
6 The Umayyad dynasty (CE 661–750) was the first of the great Sunni dynasties of caliphs of the Islamic Empire. It was succeeded by the Baghdadi Abbasid dynasty (CE 750–1258).
7 The Islamic calendar dates from the withdrawal (*hijra* or *hegira*) of Muhammad and his followers to the city of Medina in CE 622.
8 Hijaz: a region in the northwest of present-day Saudi Arabia, and the site of Islam's holy places. Evidence has been found that the Hijaz was part of the Roman province of Arabia.
9 *Mamluks*: mainly Turkic slave soldiers who converted to Islam and served the Muslim caliphs and Ottoman Empire during the middle ages. They first served the Abbasid caliphs in ninth-century Baghdad
10 The Tunisian Ibn Khaldun (CE 1332–1406), a celebrated Arab historiographer and historian, often viewed as one of the forerunners of present-day historiography, sociology and economics.

11 The Turkish Ottoman Empire existed from CE 1299 to 1923. At the height of its power, in the sixteenth and seventeenth centuries, its territory included Anatolia, the Middle East, parts of North Africa and much of Southeast Europe.

12 Born in Córdoba, Spain, Averroes (CE 1126–98) was a highly influential Andalusian-Arab philosopher and lawyer. The Persian al-Ghazali (CE 1058–1111) was one of the greatest Islamic theologians and mystical thinkers. The scholar Ibn Taymiyya (CE 1263–1328) believed that the first three generations of Islam were the best role models for Islamic life. Their *sunna*, or practice, together with the Qur'an, constituted an infallible guide to life; any deviation from their practice was to be forbidden.

13 In the naval battle of Lepanto (CE October 7 1571), a fleet of the Holy League coalition (comprising the Papacy, Spain, Venice, Genoa, and others) defeated a force of Ottoman galleys. It was one of the most decisive naval defeats in the Mediterranean.

14 On March 20 1799, Napoleon laid siege to the Mediterranean port of Acre, in present-day Israel, then ruled by the governor of Damascus Al-Jazzar. The siege failed, and Napoleon retreated two months later on May 21.

15 Khayr al-Din al-Tunisi (d.1889) was the foremost Tunisian statesman of the nineteenth century. He worked to reform government, education, and the economy. His 1867 manifesto, *The Surest Path*, addressed issues of European superiority and the importance of applying Western innovations that did not compromise Islamic precedent to strengthen the state.

16 Born in Kavala, northern Greece, Ibrahim Pasha (CE 1789–1848) was the adopted son of Muhammad Ali of Egypt. He was sent by his father to conquer Syria in 1831 after a prolonged quarrel with the Ottoman government. He took Acre, Damascus and Homs and, after a convention was signed on May 6, Syria temporarily came under Egyptian rule.

17 Rifaa al-Tahtawi (CE 1801–73) was an Egyptian social and political reformer. His highly influential book, an account of his five-year stay in Paris in the late 1820s and early 1830s, appeared in 1834.

18 A noted Arab writer and scholar, the Lebanese Butrus al-Bustani (CE 1819–83) is best known for creating the first modern Arabic encyclopaedia; he also created a dictionary and founded a number of periodicals. A Maronite Christian, he later converted to Protestantism. He was an ardent nationalist and played a decisive role in formulating the principles of Syrian nationalism.

19 Abdul Hamid II (CE 1842–1918) ruled the Ottoman Empire from August 1875 until his deposition in April 1909. In 1876 he suspended the new constitution; its author, Midhat Pasha, was exiled.

20 Jamal al-Din al-Afghani (CE 1839–97) was an anticolonial political activist, opposing foreign rule of Muslim lands.

21 Taha Hussein (CE 1889–1973) was a writer and scholar of Arabic literature, and a figurehead for the modernist movement in Egypt. The playwright Tawfiq al-Hakim (CE 1898–1987) was one of the major figures of twentieth-century Arabic literature and also played a central role in Arab political and social life. Ahmed Shawqi (CE 1868–1932) was an Egyptian poet and dramatist who was a pioneer of the modern Arabic literary movement, introducing poetic epic to the Arabic literary tradition. His poetry is considered some of the most influential of the twentieth century. The Arab–American Amin al-Rihani (CE 1876–1940) was a writer and theorist of Arab nationalism.

22 All four were influential in the development of Arab nationalism. The Yemeni-born Syrian Sati al-Husri (CE 1880–1967) was a writer and educationist; Michel Aflaq (CE 1910–89), also a Syrian, was the ideological founder of Baathism; Constantine Zurayq (CE 1909–2000) was a prominent Arab intellectual and academic; the historian Edmond Rabbath (CE 1901–1991) wrote the first nationalist history of Syria.

23 The Lebanese Antoun Saadeh (CE 1904–49) was a social nationalist thinker and founder of the Syrian Social Nationalist Party. The journalist and lawyer Ahmad Lotfi al-Sayyed (CE 1872–1963) was a prominent advocate of Egyptian modernism in the first half of the twentieth century.

24 Hassan al-Banna (CE 1906–49) was an Egyptian social and political reformer. He founded the Muslim Brotherhood.

25 The Iraqi-born Ahmed ibn Husayn al-Mutanabbi (CE 915–65) is revered as one of the greatest poets in the Arabic language.

26 Nizar Qabbani (CE 1923–98) was a Syrian diplomat and publisher, and one of the foremost contemporary poets in the Arab world.

27 Maroun Naccache (CE 1817–55), a playwright held to be the father of Lebanese, and more generally Arab, theatre.

28 The Egyptian singer and musician Om Kulthum (CE 1904–75) is one of the best-loved musicians in the Arab world.

29 Sayyed Darwish (CE 1892–1923), an Alexandrian singer and composer whose work is held to symbolise the shift from an elitist Ottoman music to a national Egyptian style.

30 Hoda Shaarawi (CE 1879–1947) was a pioneering Egyptian feminist and nationalist who remains the figurehead of the women's liberation movement in Egypt.

31 July Monarchy: the reign of Louis Philippe, last king of France, from July 1830 to February 1848, when the Second Republic was proclaimed.

32 *Tsahal*: an abbreviation of Haganah LeYisrael, the Israeli armed forces, or IDF. The Haganah was previously a Jewish paramilitary organization in the British Mandate of Palestine, and was the main precursor to the Israeli army.

33 Sayyid Mawdudi (CE 1903–79) was one of the twentieth century's most influential Islamic theologians, and founder of the Pakistani Islamic political party, the Jamaat-e-Islami. His ideas profoundly influenced Sayyid Qutb (CE 1906–66), the Egyptian Islamist intellectual and author, closely associated with the Muslim Brotherhood.

34 One of Egypt's most prominent activists, Professor Saad Eddin Ibrahim was director of a Cairo research institute that monitored elections and was at times critical of the Egyptian government. In summer 2000 he was arrested, along with twenty-seven colleagues, found guilty and jailed. Professor Ibrahim was sentenced to seven years in prison; he was finally acquitted of all charges and released in March 2003.